The church ought to be the most creative place on the planet. We're called to be trend-setters and culture-creators and if we are going to reach emerging generations, we've got to utilize emerging technologies to get our message across. The ideas and thoughts shared in this book have influenced the way churches around the country, including National Community Church, have redeemed technology and communication and used it to serve God's eternal purposes. Outspoken: Conversations on Church Communication is a must-read for church leaders who are discerning how to leverage new media to reach more people with the gospel.

Mark Batterson

Lead Pastor,
National Community Church
Washington D.C.

How do you interact and communicate with church leaders and attendees? This book will challenge your daily practices and invite you into a rich, ongoing conversation about the importance of effective communication in the church.

Beth Dahlenburg

Executive Director, Marketing,
Willow Creek Association

The Center for Church Communication's passion for the Church and communication is crystal clear in Outspoken. This is a must-read if you are in church communications. I guarantee the collection of over 60 unique contributors from all different backgrounds will inspire you, and challenge you...it did me!

Terry Storch
LifeChurch.tv
YouVersion

Finally, a resource that gives the church the necessary tools to effectively tell its story! With Outspoken, Tim Schraeder brings together a who's who of church communication experts to offer practical ideas and insights that any church, regardless of size, culture or location, can access and apply to their individual context. Outspoken is a huge gift to the church.

Lindy Lowry
Editor of Outreach magazine

Published by the Center for Church Communication
Los Angeles, California
www.CFCCLabs.org

ISBN: 146373817X
EAB-13: 978-1463738174

Printed by CreateSpace in the United States of America

To our fellow strugglers.

Table of Contents

*"There's nowhere in Africa we don't go. We go
to every town, every village, every community,
every township."*

—Coca-Cola CEO

In a recent issue of *Bloomberg Businessweek*, Duane Stanford
tells the story of Coca-Cola and the intense focus they have to
penetrate Africa with the gospel of Coke: "Like Alexander the
Great, at the prospect of having no worlds left to conquer…
Coca-Cola will rely on some of the poorest nations to generate
the 7 to 9 percent earnings growth it has promised investors."

Piles of trash are burning outside the Mamakamau Shop in Uthiru,
a suburb of Nairobi, Kenya. Sewage trickles by in an open trench.
Across the street, a worker at a bar gets ready for the lunch rush
by scraping the hair off a couple of roasted goat heads. It's about
70 degrees, the sun is beating down, it smells like decay and it's
time for Coke to move some product. Annual per capita consumption of Coca-Cola in Kenya is 39 servings. In more developed coun-
tries like Mexico, which consumes more Coca-Cola than any other
country, it runs 665 servings per year. One does not need an MBA
to see the possibilities.

Coke could have focused on China (too complicated) and/or India
(Pepsi already has a strong presence), where there is also plenty
of potential, but they decided to increase its focus on Africa, where
Coke has been since 1929. "Coke plans to spend $12 billion in the
continent during the next 10 years, more than twice as much as in
the previous decade."

Muhtar Kent, CEO of Coca-Cola, says "There's nowhere in Africa that we don't go. Being in a country is very easy, you can go and set up a depot in every capital city. That's not what we're about. We go to every town, every village, every community, every township."

Coke's mission is clear, and they won't let geography stop them. In much of Africa, it's a challenge to deliver product over poor roads, through large crowds and in the grueling heat. Their first rule is to get the product "cold and close." There is 65 percent unemployment inside one township of 500,000 in Johannesburg, South Africa. No problem for Coke. In 2009, they stocked the streets with drink coolers and Coke signage. "To keep the coolers full, the [local] bottler extended credit to merchants who didn't have the capital to take on inventory, giving them seven days to pay."

Coke is so focused on reaching Africa, they go to great lengths to help communities beyond just generating and satisfying their thirst.

> Ann Kimeu, 34, sips Sprite through a straw from a green glass bottle. A few blocks away, residents of the slum, which has no public water or sewer system, pay 3 shillings to fill used 20-liter cooking oil jugs with fresh water from a Coke sponsored well. At a new bathroom Coke is helping to build in the poorest section of the slum, it will cost 2 shillings to use the toilet or the shower. Kimeu buys soft drinks as many as four times a week. It's not a treat. She's mostly just thirsty. A seamstress, Kimeu earns about 1,000 Kenya shillings ($12) a week when business is good. At 35 shillings a bottle, the soft drinks consume 14 percent or more of her income.

If Coke will go to such great lengths to reach a continent with sugar water, what will it take for us to reach across the street and around the block with the transforming story of the gospel? May I suggest that it will not be through fancy signage, gorgeous buildings, attractive graphics or mesmerizing experiences? It won't be through Facebook, Twitter or the next big social platform. All of these things might help; but the one thing, more than any other, that will secure the attention and affection of the outsider is the generous hospitality of a spirit-led life.

Coke understands that the closer it gets to homes, the closer it gets to hearts. It would be difficult not to welcome Coke into your life when it's right outside your door!

Coke cares less about you coming to Coke and more about you caring for Coke. In the same way, may we as communicators represent the life of Christ in a way that attempts not to bring people into our world, but instead moves us to dwell among outsiders in a way that is authentic, loving and purposefully present.

Two thousand years ago God cared so much for this world he created, that he sent his son to dwell among us. To show us back to God. To show us the way home.

As you read and reflect on these outspoken voices and stories, I pray you will have an increasing love for the outsider, and a relentless determination to go to them, be with them and show them the way home.

Brad Abare is the founder of the Center for Church Communication and serves as the board chair. He consults with organizations that are in the midst of significant transition.

Web: BradAbare.com

It's been said that Christianity is fundamentally a communication event. All throughout the history of mankind, God has desired to communicate and have a relationship with us. From the early stories recorded in our Bible where he used burning bushes, miraculous signs and the voices of prophets to speak to men, to the days when he became a man and dwelled among us, God has longed to communicate with each and every one of us.

The early church didn't have the modern technologies we have today. There were no billboards or direct mail campaigns to announce Jesus was coming. The disciples didn't tweet or blog the Sermon on the Mount or other messages Jesus gave during his ministry. The one thing the early church did have, however, was captivating stories worth telling. People couldn't help but tell their friends and family all that they had seen and heard, and proclaim the redemptive work of Christ and the hope of the gospel.

In Jesus' final words to his disciples, we were all called to go and tell the message of the gospel. Jesus promised the Holy Spirit, which would give us the power to be witnesses for him in our cities, nations and to the ends of the earth. From a dramatic moment in Acts 2, when the Holy Spirit came and 3,000 people came to know Christ in a single day, the redemptive work has not stopped and the church has continued to grow every single day as people have shared the story and the message of Christ. A lot has changed since then.

The church is credited with saving the arts in the dark ages. The church used art as a primary way to share and communicate the gospel using images in a world that was largely illiterate. From detailed frescos to intricate stained glass windows, to awe inspiring domes of cathedrals, the church used the arts to tell its story and communicate the message of the gospel.

When Gutenberg invented the printing press, the Bible—which had largely been unavailable to anyone—became accessible to everyone. This opened the doors to opportunities that were never available before and fueled the Reformation, which gave birth to many of our modern-day church movements.

Church historians have noted that with every major cultural revolution that has taken place in modern times, there's been an accompanying movement of God's Spirit as the church has found new ways to reach more people. Our message has never changed but the way we communicate it has found new forms and new mediums throughout the generations.

Today we stand on the forefront of a new cultural revolution. The ways we interact and communicate are changing literally every day. It has been said that more data will be created in the next four years than in the entire history of the world. Through bits, bytes, tweets and push notifications, the way we share our stories has changed dramatically. The way we interact and share information has found new forms and the very definition of things like friendship and community have new meaning as we connect and are "friends" with people we've never even met face-to-face.

In the midst of this massive new revolution stands the church.

Jesus said that he would build his church and nothing would prevail against it, and in the changing and adaptive times we live in, we carry with us the sacred privilege of sharing a timeless, unchanging story in an ever-changing world. We, as the church, have never been as equipped or resourced to communicate the message of the gospel as we are today. With this amazing opportunity comes a tremendous responsibility. We have a moment and time in history to steward the opportunity and resources God has given us to communicate his story. We are literally able to reach millions of people around the globe with the click of a mouse. Our content has never been more widely accessible and our message is one that desperately needs to be heard.

Marketing isn't a term that is found in our Bible and to some it may seem odd to lump the idea of church and traditional marketing together. However, at its core, the ideas of marketing are very central to how our faith has grown throughout the years. In today's world, marketing is defined by many as being the sum total of everything a business or organization does. How a business does business has marketing implications. For the sake of this book, we chose to define marketing in the context of the church as communication. Everything our churches do today forms the message we are ultimately communicating to the world. As the ways we interact and engage continue to change, the role of communication will only become more vital to the life of the church.

Every single day in churches all around the world men and women are charged with the responsibility of leading communication for their churches. Whether it's by laying out bulletins, writing content, designing graphics, editing video or posting content to websites, these people are influencing the way their churches interact and communicate to the outside world, extending timeless truth into a hyper-connected world.

This book is a collection of thoughts, ideas and principles that are shaping and inspiring the way some outspoken church communications leaders are leading communication in their churches, from churches of 25 to 25,000, from Des Moines, Iowa, to Sydney, Australia. Throughout these pages you'll be challenged to think through how your church is communicating and consider new ways of thinking. The end goal of this book is to engage you in an ongoing conversation about the role of communication in the church.

It is our prayer that these thoughts will frustrate, educate and motivate you and your church to communicate, with uncompromising clarity, the truth of Jesus.

Tim Schraeder has over 10 years of experience leading communications in churches. He is a communications consultant and was previously the director of communications at Park Community Church in Chicago. He's also the instigator of this project and the co-director of the Center for Church Communication.

Web: TimSchraeder.com
Twitter: @TimSchraeder

GENERAL COMMUNICATION

There is a common misconception that preaching is something that happens only from behind a pulpit on the weekend. This is narrow-minded. Who says that is the only way the gospel can be communicated?

Tradition may say so, but even the most set-in-our-ways among us have shaken off this notion unknowingly. The Bible Belt church whose sign you can see in an ironic gallery online is preaching from their signage in the parking lot. They would probably even tell you so.

Every time you communicate anything in any medium as a church, it is preaching. I'm not suggesting you start tweeting, "God reads knee-mail," from your church's account. What I am suggesting is that no matter what you're saying, it is a sermon being preached.

When you inform your community of a free outreach with no strings attached, you preach of God's generosity. When you pains-takingly craft a design for a sermon series, you preach of God's beauty and preach the content to visual learners in a way a sermon would not speak to them. When you package a video of someone's testimony, you are preaching of God's redemption.

It is all preaching.

You should feel encouraged by this. What you're doing is important. It is very important. You may feel that you toil in vain. You might want to quit. You may feel that you are putting in late nights and long hours for no reason because, "who cares about a stupid sermon graphic anyway?" Nothing could be further from the truth. You are preaching the gospel.

The question we must ask ourselves, then, is whether or not we are treating what we do with the level of reverence that it deserves. We would be appalled to learn that our pastor had thrown a sermon together at the last minute without seeking the face of our Father. How many times have we done this with our work in media, design or communication?

We ought to be spending time in the Bible, bathing our work in prayer, caring for it as though it has the potential to radically alter lives.

Because it does.

Jeremy Sexton is a pastor, speaker, artist and filmmaker. He works at National Community Church in Washington, D.C

Web: JeremySexton.net
Twitter: @JeremySexton

Communication in the church, what a brilliant thought.

Communication *and* the church... even better!

To me, the word 'communication' or 'marketing' is so much deeper than a strategically placed logo, some quirky artwork or a catchy phrase. It is the tool into which we can breathe life, stir a thought, bring inspiration and make something that is otherwise difficult to understand, clear and relevant. Now take that idea and add it to the church—both internally with how we communicate our message to followers of Christ and externally with how we communicate the gospel to our community. What an amazing responsibility!

I believe that our art, our brochures, our online media, our print media and all of our 'communications' should be bringing God the glory he deserves. When we strive for excellence in everything we do, then we not only honor God with our output, but our input.

1. Communicating Jesus' bride is an honor; it is a privilege we should never take for granted. We have a great responsibility to communicate *truth*. Don't shy away from having God factors! (Spiritual I know!) Jesus is attractive, the Bible is the living, breathing word of God and it speaks truth, turns on lights in dark places and gives hope in the most hopeless situations. So why wouldn't you use Scriptures that speak to the soul? As Christians, the Bible is our greatest source of inspiration. Let's remember, we are not communicating the message or mission statement of any old corporation or community center— **we are communicating the church.**

2. It's all for *him*! (Enough said.)

3. Don't just check a box. Think outside of it. It's really easy under pressure to just 'get the job done.' But I dare you, challenge you and urge you to be different. Step outside of the box! The church is alive, it is moving forward and the kingdom of God is advancing like we've never seen. Don't let communication be stale and stagnate by doing the same thing over and over and using common and predictable ideas. You have a responsibility to make the church shine! Make it loving, fresh, attractive, warm and welcoming.

Paint the right picture!

4. Lastly, "Whatever your hand finds to do, do it with all your might." -Ecclesiastes 9:10

Whether you are involved in the day-to-day outworking of communication in your church, the creative input or the administration of the department, God says *this* is a form of worship. Bring your absolute best to the team. If you want good design: read, learn, surround yourself with good design! If you're not passionate or inspired, ask God to give you a passion! Open your hands and have a soft heart and a listening ear; become a tool where God can use you and I promise that the more that you understand the creator, the more and more God will enlarge your thinking, take you to the next level and breathe fresh, innovative *creativity* in and through you.

Jay Argaet is the art director and head of communications at Hillsong Church in Sydney, Australia.

Twitter: @JArgaet

God wired me to dream big. When fellow brainstormers ask, "How could we ever pull that off?" I know we're right where he wants us to be.

Where's the excitement in having it all figured out anyway? Where's the need for God?

We're fast to discredit the weird and out-of-the-box ideas that come to us in the shower, our drive home from work, etc., but God speaks in those moments. Don't ignore them.

Ultimately, these dreams are the basis for what Seth Godin calls, "remarkable experiences."

You want to reach more people in your community? It doesn't take throwing a lot of budget at fancy communication and marketing pieces—they'll find their place. It just takes a remarkable experience that engages the community and gets your regulars excited about inviting their friends and family.

Can I let you in on a secret? Remarkable only takes one ask.

Case in point, the pre-Easter event we held at all of the Chapel campuses, Kids' Day. We were looking for a bigger draw than just inflatables and face painting.

My family and I are big fans of Nickelodeon's *iCarly*. Just by happenstance, I found out that actor Noah Munck who plays the character Gibby is a Christian. God immediately put it on my heart that we needed to bring that guy to Chicago for Kids' Day.

After a little digging I found that Noah's dad, Greg, is on staff at an awesome church in California. I sent a quick e-mail and he responded with excitement that we wanted Noah to help with a kingdom event.

Greg had Noah's agent get in touch with me, we sealed the deal and it was on.

Here are the numbers across all five of our campuses:

- 4,000 people in attendance including children, students and adults.
- Over 2,000 people walked into the Chapel for the first time.
- Over 2,000 clicks from Facebook ads—it's easy to market remarkable.

What's your "ask"?

My dad used to say "the answer is always no 'til you ask."

What "ask" is holding your God-sized idea back from reality? What's crazy enough to start a buzz and make people want to walk through your church doors?

The best part is looking back after a remarkable experience, seeing the complexity and wondering how you ever did it.

You didn't.

Cleve Persinger is the founder of Creative Missions and MediaSalt.com. He also serves on staff at The Chapel in Chicagoland.
Web: MediaSalt.com
Twitter: @Persinger

My friend and mentor Mark Pierson (a worship curator from New Zealand) wrote something very profound:

> *"The answer to the church's problems doesn't lie in greater creativity or better music or more relevance or a better understanding of culture or even the arts. The solution lies in asking better questions. Or at least that's where we need to start."*

He goes on to write that one of the best questions you can ask when producing something is, "What do you want to say?"—not only in your content, but also in your context. The truth is, we are communicating even when we are not "communicating."

Let's take a live worship gathering, for instance. (I'll use this as my example because it's the world in which I work as a VJ.) For many years, my main focus has been solely on the content of the video screens. I like to expand people's minds and hearts during worship by VJing various images, colors, textures and video clips in such a way that leads them in worship, just like our songs are intended to do. I want to use the screens as a mirror that reflects the glory of God. So I hold closely to the old mantra: "Content is king!"

Only in recent years have I begun to look beyond the screens and to look at the worship environment more holistically, asking the same question: "What do I want to say?" This has led to some shifting values in my philosophical approach to leading worship. And I've started to realize that the power and influence of the environment (context) has been vastly underestimated and worse yet, ignored. You see, your environment communicates to people what you value as a church.

So in Mark's words, I view myself as a "maker of context" rather than just a "presenter of content." I want to shift my approach away from "communicating at" my people and toward "communicating with or among" my people.

Some examples of how I do this: Changing the seating arrangement, focal points of the room, content of the screens, house lighting levels and incorporating environmental projection. I want to wrap the entire room in as much creativity as I do the stage. I want to say *visually* that the congregation is just as important as the leaders on the stage.

When people encounter your church (whether in the building, in the community or online), what is the environment they are stepping into, and what do you want to say.

Stephen Proctor is a visual worship pioneer. He creates environments with his company Grateful Inconvenience.
Web: WorshipVJ.com
Twitter: @WorshipVJ

"How to Dress for Success" columns are an editorial staple in men's fashion magazines. Amid cologne samples and perfectly coifed pompadours, writers offer their stylistic expertise. Trousers are to be tailored; shirts should fit the form rather than flap in the wind; and it's not completely girly for a man to carry a bag. These principles are accompanied by images of Average Joe going from frumpy to dashing across a two-page spread. It's all about fit.

Some churches are slim—some churches are husky.

The church communications team has an incredible responsibility to select its church's wardrobe; all things viewed, read, clicked, heard and touched by the public. But like men with hairy necks and ill-fitting suits reading fashion magazines, how does one know what fits?

As a former textologist who helped broaden church communication through text messaging, churches would inquire about the best mobile executions. Conversations always began like this: "Tell me about your church."

Replies often revolved around weekly attendance, technological inventory and a ready-to-launch sermon series. Beyond the necessary tactical answers, the best responses were always quantitative and qualitative.

If church leaders know the pulse of their congregations, then they are best equipped to serve them.

Creative teams must decide if social networking, podcasting, webcasting or mobile integration helps or hurts their communication strategy. Understanding the church both inside and outside sanctuary walls is crucial to recognizing what fits.

Understand the Demo

The beautiful thing about church communication is that the congregation is a living body; not a target market or demographic report. Remember that all exchanges between church and body should be a human experience.

Know the Trends

Being familiar with the media consumption tendencies of your church can best shape the relevance of where to meet your congregation. For example, it might make sense to launch mobile initiatives if your audience is constantly texting during the sermon.

Be a Datahead

Optimize your communication performance by pulling data on executions. Are people visiting, clicking, following, friending, viewing, downloading or streaming? If not, perhaps it's best to focus on what's working and stop spinning your wheels elsewhere.

Avoid "Shiny New Toy Syndrome"

Just because a groundbreaking technology emerges to market doesn't necessarily mean that it will revolutionize your church for the better. Strategically think through how it might fit the needs of the people you lead.

Church communications folks are responsible for dressing and tailoring what is worn by the church and encountered by the congregation. You decide what fits.

Michael Forsberg lives in Chicago and works in advertising. He likes Pad Thai, skinny jeans and bear hugs.

Web: MichaelForsberg.tumblr.com
Twitter: @MichaelForsberg

᷿67 film *Cool Hand Luke*, an outraged warden lashes out against an insubordinate prisoner, striking him in the face. The warden regains his composure and utters the now famous phrase, "What we've got here is a failure to communicate."

The warden believed that the root cause was the prisoner's failure to understand what he was saying. In a similar vein, many of the issues we face on a daily basis...

- issues at home, at the church or at the office;
- issues between our family, friends and coworkers;
- issues meeting project deadlines and deliverables;
- issues with authority, responsibilities and commitments;
- issues related to misunderstandings, misinterpretations and mistakes;

...can often be traced back to poor, ineffective and untimely communication.

The church has often struggled to master the art of communication—from within its four walls, from the church to its congregation, from the congregation to the church and from members to members. Thankfully the communication issues that churches face can easily be addressed with some basic education and planning.

Following are some simple principles that should be applied to every form of communication. This includes everything, such as e-mails to a small group, invitations to an event or ministry, the church website, the printed worship program, graphics on the video screens and in-person announcements.

1. What

The first step is to fully understand what you are being asked to communicate. Find out the **story** that is driving the communication. For example, don't simply announce that Vacation Bible School is next month and assume everyone understands the benefits. Instead, explain the positive impact that it will have on the lives of the children and volunteers. Include testimonials from those involved in prior years.

2. Who

Next, consider the **audience**. Tailor your message to the specific audience that truly needs to hear it. If your church is conducting a class specifically for new parents, then customize the message so it speaks directly to their needs.

3. How

When developing your message keep it **simple**. Don't use the cryptic language only some Christians may understand. Explain in simple, every day terms how one can come to know and trust in Jesus rather than inviting them to be "washed in the sanctifying blood of the Lamb." Your message should also be crystal **clear**. Reduce the effort to get involved with an event or ministry to no more than three or four easy to understand steps and direct them to the first step.

4. Where

Now that you know the story you need to determine which **channels** should be used to best reach your intended audience. In some instances an e-mail to a small group is sufficient. In other instances, you may need to spread the word on your website, Twitter, Facebook and in the worship announcements. Keep in mind that the members of your congregation are bombarded with hundreds of messages each day. Don't add to the noise by communicating every idea, event or program to everyone.

Curtis Simmons is the vice president of marketing and community for Fellowship Technologies.

Web: DailyConcern.com
Twitter: @CurtisSimmons

Curtis Simmons just shared some simple and direct ideas that can keep your church from having a failure to communicate. It's good advice. He took what's become a cliché quote at face value, but in the movie *Cool Hand Luke* there was something deeper going on. The prisoner, Luke, wasn't suffering from a failure to communicate, but a failure to connect. As churches trying to communicate, we need to avoid simple miscommunication—yes!—but we also need to realize that it's about more than communication.

Luke certainly understood the warden's words. Understanding the words—communication—wasn't the problem. The problem went deeper. The words didn't connect with Luke. He had a lifelong problem with authority. He wasn't the prisoner to toe the line, do his time and move on.

It really didn't matter what the warden said or how he said it. It didn't matter what methods or tactics he employed. It didn't matter how often or for how long they forced Luke to spend the night in the box. Luke was going to escape anyway, consequences be damned.

Churches should make every effort to communicate clearly so we can avoid simple failures, as Curtis rightly suggests. But we should also recognize these deeper "failures to communicate" that keep lost sheep lost. What a tragedy it would be if the church had perfect communication but failed to connect with people's hearts.

And this is why, as communicators, we're truly reliant on God. We can do everything possible to communicate clearly and still miss the mark. That is when we truly are reminded that God controls everything and we can't do this in our own power.

Luke didn't need better communication. He needed connection. He needed someone to intervene in his life. He needed God to open his heart. That's why the climactic scene of the movie finds Luke in a clapboard country church, looking up to the rafters and calling out to God.

We need to remember that clearer and better communication is great, but it's not everything. Sometimes it takes something more. Sometimes it requires going the extra mile to break through and connect with a fellow soul. And sometimes it's out of our hands. As the warden says in exasperation, "Some men you just can't reach." And we can't. All of our efforts in outspoken communication ultimately come down to a higher power.

Kevin D. Hendricks lives in St. Paul, Minn., and works as a freelance writer and editor. He wrote the book *Addition by Adoption: Kids, Causes & 140 Characters*.

Web: KevinDHendricks.com
Twitter: @KevinHendricks

There's one thing I've figured out about multi-site church communication: I'm never going to have it all figured out. Talking to peers at other churches has convinced me I'm not alone in this.

Though it's an ever-shifting landscape, there's a common thread. At a central level, it's impossible to write, see, touch, edit or review all of the communication that happens on multiple sites.

I've officially waved the white flag of surrender on controlling, containing or otherwise keeping a lid on the entirety of our communication. Embracing that limitation gives me the freedom to be more effective in what I can do:

Connect
In conversations with our teams lately, I'm asking questions like: What's going on in your ministry? What communication challenges are you facing? How can I help? It might mean a new to-do item, but occasionally helping is as easy as pointing them to someone who's figured out a similar problem.

Align
I'm on the lookout for larger patterns, like opportunities we might be missing or potential communication traffic jams where everybody wants to promote their programs at the same time. I don't solve these issues by myself. Instead, I ask questions and pull people together so we can coordinate instead of compete: plan ahead instead of react.

Coach
When a piece misses the mark, it's time to course-correct. These aren't "you're doing it wrong," conversations, but look more like this: "If I understand your goal correctly (paraphrase it), here's

a way we might be able to reach it more effectively..." It helps to have regular evaluation spot-checks built in to your schedule.

Train
Creating proactive and documented training equips new (or newly interested) team members. Some ideas: Notes and slides for a talk about effective communication, a recorded group book discussion, a style guide that includes best practices, a collection of links to great blog posts and helpful resources, etc.

Resource
Writing global content and standard blurbs that our campuses can grab and tweak to fit their needs makes their lives easier, while raising the content quality and reducing the duplication of effort across locations.

Trust
I'm never going to understand a community as well their campus team. They are the experts in their audience—they know their stories and their struggles. Communication shouldn't look the same at every location, but should be tailored to their culture. So once I've done everything above, I let it go and trust that our teams will know best how to communicate the love of Christ to the people in their community.

Lori Bailey is the director of communications at LifeChurch.tv.

Web: LoriBailey.com

Twitter: @LoriBailey

Church communication is marked by a huge dilemma: talent without subject. It doesn't matter how gifted, strategic or innovative you are as a communicator if your subject is missing. Without a primary message, you have nothing. Imagine a hot dog stand with only condiments, not meat.

Most leadership teams of our effective, creative churches have not articulated the unifying essence of their organization:

- What is the heartbeat of your church?
- What can your church do better than 10,000 others?
- How do we uniquely make disciples in our corner of the world?

Problem #1: When you showed up, the core content probably wasn't clear.

Problem #2: There were plenty of urgent needs that got you busy pretty quick.

Therefore the church communicator is left trafficking in minor messages:

- The next sermon series promotion.
- The top five announcements this Sunday.
- The children's ministry piece.

We spend all of our time on background vocals with no vocalist. Less clutter is beautiful if the core is clear. Less noise is fantastic, if you have a song to sing. Tactics are important, but they are your own enemy if the subject isn't identified.

Today, your subject is in one of three places.

First, your subject may be in clear view but not communicated. This "creative's dilemma" happens by creating new stuff for creativity's sake. The great American artist, Andrew Wyeth, speaks to this tendency: "Most artists have to find something fresh to paint. Frankly I find that quite boring. I would much rather find fresh meaning in something already familiar." Solve this dilemma by pushing through to the genius of the artist—think outside the box, inside the big idea. Stay on subject.

Second, your subject may be forgotten. Half buried, your work now is that of the treasure hunter who shows others the location of the lost gold mine. Help other leaders rediscover. Align everything you do to reveal and support it.

Finally, your subject may be unidentified. This is common and puts you in the most challenging position. You must "lead up," encourage and inspire the team to work a discernment process. Don't harass leaders about what's wrong. Focus on the opportunity to take the church and all communication to another level.

Don't be a Picasso with a missing subject. You are too talented, life is too short and the mission of Jesus is too important.

Will Mancini is the founder of Auxano.com and the author of *Church Unique*. He coaches pastors on how to discover, develop and deliver compelling vision from core identity to visual brand.

Web: WillMancini.com
Twitter: @WillMancini

There's a word that has generated lots of momentum in the church world in recent years. It's a word that gets thrown around frequently in conferences, workshops, staff teams and blogs. We've become obsessed with it. The word? Excellence.

Excellence has become a mantra behind much of the work we do. We've attempted to prove wrong the world's assumption that if it's Christian, it's sub-par. Excellence is a value that has often been overlooked in the church, and it's as important as ever to keep it at the core of everything we do.

However, as we've focused our attention on the value of excellence, we may have lost our focus on what makes our message truly effective. It's a disturbing trend that I didn't see coming until I witnessed it with my own eyes.

In an effort to demand excellence in all that we do, a more important principle has been overlooked. That principle is authenticity.

At West Ridge Church, we recently put a lot of time, effort and money into a video and print piece outlining an exciting new initiative. We spent a significant number of hours thinking through the technical details of the script, lighting, shots, design and all the other pieces that are important to us for a project done with excellence. In the end, we were satisfied with the final product. It was done with excellence.

So, was that enough?

Interestingly, we generated a much higher response out of the secondary communication strategies we implemented. Things like webcam videos, simple blog posts and in-service testimonies seemed to be more effective than the polished video and print pieces. The difference? The more the authenticity of the person, message or story shined, the more effective the result.

Could it be that people place much greater value than we realized on connecting and identifying with the message rather than the quality of the delivery? If so, it may be time to redefine excellence.

So when you build your new website, dream up a new video or design a brochure, begin with authenticity. Focus on sharing the unique story and passion of your church. Focus on creating meaningful conversations. Focus on developing an authentic picture of the heart of your church. Focus less on how cool your church is and more on how you're a church full of authentic people, struggling with real problems, living out a day-by-day relationship with Jesus Christ together.

When it comes to communication: Make excellence a value, make authenticity a mandate.

Phil Bowdle is the communications director at West Ridge Church near Atlanta. He creates high-impact experiences through communications that lead people to Jesus.

Web: PhilBowdle.com
Twitter: @PhilBowdle

In a series of articles I recently discovered, *ThisIsInspired* magazine is exploring the Seven Principles of Japanese Aesthetics. The first article introduced a term I was not familiar with: Kanso

かんそ

Kanso means "simplicity and/or elimination of clutter." The article explains that by definition, Kanso is when things are expressed in a simple, natural manner. But Kanso must be thought of beyond merely decoration. More importantly, it refers to clarity—a clarity that emerges by removing everything that is non-essential. By doing so, you create greater accessibility.

The article actually applies the concept to web design (good advice if you are in that process now). It occurred to me that it is also an important concept to apply across all organizational communication. Often, there are so many competing and inconsistent messages that what is seen, heard and experienced on a week-to-week basis only creates confusion. The competing messages actually become roadblocks to our messages being received. Essentially, the complexity tunes people out.

If you want to reach people and get them talking about the essence of who you are, make yourself accessible. Practice Kanso.

Keep in mind that this is about simplification as opposed to over-simplification. People want and need identity, context, cues and understanding to establish relationship with your brand -- with you.

Here are a few thoughts to help you get started:

- Eliminate competing and non-essential messages.

- Maintain consistency across all of your communications.

- Inspire by reinforcing your vision through every sensory experience.

- Kanso.

Cheryl Marting is the chief connections officer at Auxano, a church consulting group.

Web: EverythingSpeaks.com
Twitter: @CherylMarting

Not too long ago, my wife bought a board game from Target. It was one of those 10-in-1 games—backgammon, checkers, chess, Chinese checkers, etc. She showed me the box when she got home. It looked really nice, especially since it was only $10. It was a nice wood set. Very polished and looked to be pretty sturdy. Then, we opened it up.

It was the ugliest piece of junk ever. It was nothing more than flimsy cardboard and plastic. The Chinese checkers didn't even use marbles. They were small plastic discs that looked like poker chips. We looked at the box again, trying to see any similarities between what was on the box and what was in the box. No similarities were found. Then I looked for fine print that said some something along the lines of "actual product may vary from picture." Didn't find that either.

It was a blatant misrepresentation. It wasn't what was advertised.

Have you ever seen a church misrepresent itself in that same fashion? Often, churches look very enticing. They advertise themselves as having a world-class children's ministry, dynamic worship and life changing teaching. But in reality the world-class children's ministry is nothing more than volunteer childcare, dynamic worship is singing praise and worship songs from the early 90s, life-changing teaching is moving from the KJV to the New KJV.

That kind of advertising not only hurts that church, but it impacts all of us trying to bring about life change to our culture. Why should they believe us? They've heard promises from churches that didn't deliver.

Often, we project who we want to be in our advertising. That's not advertising, that's vision casting. The world doesn't care about who we want to be. They care about who we are. They want to know if we can meet their needs.

Instead of over promising, we should focus on what we're good at right now.

Bobby Chandler is the director of communications at Sugar Creek Baptist Church in Sugar Land, Texas and founder of ChurchKreatives.com.

Web: ChurchKreatives.com
Twitter: @BobbyChandler

I go to an Episcopal church. We have liturgy. Our pews aren't padded. We don't do Powerpoint. We don't have a visitor's welcome center. Our website? Kinda lame. Our communications budget? A single line item for a phone book ad, which we cut. A communications committee has started and failed multiple times in the last five years.

We're what you call a normal church. One of the little guys.

I say that so you understand I'm not from one of these cutting edge churches with communications directors and flat panel TVs and sermon graphics. We've got an admin assistant, and Janice puts together a mean newsletter.

So understand where I'm coming from when I say this: There's hope for the little guy.

The people in this book talk a big talk. And many of them walk the walk. But for us little guys, it's a little overwhelming. They're debating microsites and we're still high-fiving that we even have a website.

But don't let that scare you away. Don't let that intimidate you.

The truth is you're already communicating. Don't let the fact that you're little stop you from making it better.

Here are some ways the little guy can step it up:

Make a Plan

Every time my church starts a new communications effort, whether it's a new website or a new logo, it gets mired down and mucked up.

Why? Because we have no plan. Before you talk designs or even methods, start with the basics. Who are you? Why are you communicating? What are you going to say? Who does the work?

Baby Steps

We little guys are no megachurch. We're not ready to tweet and blog and podcast. So start small. Make one steady, consistent, maintainable improvement at a time. Baby steps to the website. Baby steps to bulletins without typos. Baby steps to ditching clipart. Good communication is like a light guiding you in the darkness: It can't flare up and fade out, it has to burn slow and steady through the night.

Find a Champion

What we little guys really lack is dedicated people power. We have no staff. Janice is a rock star of an admin assistant, but her job description is six pages long. She makes the church run, she doesn't have time to moonlight as a communications director. So find champions. For each new project, find a champion who will love it, run with it and win. Show them the plan, give them some direction and empower them to make their own decisions (and their own mistakes).

Do Something

The biggest killer of progress is a lack of progress. If you don't get anywhere you'll discourage and dishearten your volunteers and you'll be starting over again. Adopt the mindset of a startup and do it quick and cheap. Make it better as you go, but make sure you're going. Don't wait for perfection.

Ignore the Dissent

We little guys invented "that's how we've always done it." Change is scary (try suggesting PowerPoint). So as your champion is getting something done with baby steps all according to plan, it's inevitable that someone will cry out "Facebook is the devil!" And now it's time to let the dissenters down easy. Change is a comin' and this little guy may be little, but he's going to communicate well. Don't let dissent grind you down.

Little Guys Can Do Big Things
So remember the story of Junior Asparagus in the VeggieTales version of David and Goliath: "He's big! But God's bigger! … With his help little guys can do big things too!"

We may be small, but we're not out.

We may not be rock stars, but we can still sing.

We may be little guys, but we've got the same grand story.

And we can tell it well.

Kevin D. Hendricks lives in St. Paul, Minn., and works as a free-lance writer and editor. He wrote the book *Addition by Adoption: Kids, Causes & 140 Characters*.

Web: KevinDHendricks.com
Twitter: @KevinHendricks

Strange title, I know, given this is a book on church communication, but hear me out.

The work of communicating in your church is... well, work and it is extremely organic. I wish we could give you all the details you need in a book, but truth is the words I am writing will probably be somewhat insufficient before the ink dries (or the e-book downloads).

All the stuff that is written on blogs, in policy manuals, communicated through design standards and even—gasp—written in books, is static. Life is organic. Static can't zig when the world zags, it does not know the community that you live in, it was not written through the lens of your senior leadership's personality (good or bad).

So here is the deal: You are going have to work and work hard to communicate your story. This book will have no quick fixes and no template formulas on 10 simple ways to communicate everything.

But here are a couple of things (static as they are) that maybe can be used to communicate the gospel through your organic story:

1. Know Who You Are Communicating To
I know this is elementary but apparently we all are not smarter than a fifth grader. Methods that work for some other community will not work with your community. You'll fail.

2. Know What You Are Communicating
Is it the gospel or is it an attempt to communicate something else? What is your goal? Why are we printing it, sending it, filming it, singing it, saying it or miming it (please e-mail me if your church has video of mime by the way—must see)?

3. Know When to Communicate

Noise and dissonance is created by sound at inappropriate time and inappropriate levels. Research, study, ask and then pray about when to communicate—don't just be a resounding cymbal and noise.

4. Rewrite This Book

Seriously, take notes and make it organic. See how your community changes what we say. Dare to use highlighters when necessary and black markers often—we reserve the right to be wrong.

Life is not sitting still and it certainly is not a policy. Love people more than policy and love the organic nature of this life. Now go rewrite this book as you write your story.

Shawn Wood is a pastor trying to communicate well to all involved. He's the lead pastor of Freedom Church.

Web: ShawnWoodWrites.com
Twitter: @ShawnWood

LEADERSHIP

OK, let's just get straight to the point here. There is a gap. Or perhaps orifice is a better word for it. And sometimes it's huge. [Insert uncomfortable pause.] Actually, on second thought, let's go back to using the word "gap."

This gap I'm referring to is the one that often exists in the relationship between a senior pastor and the church communications team. And the divide is a real problem—especially when you consider what's truly at stake.

Prior to becoming a lead pastor, I had the privilege of spending quite a bit of time working in the area of church communication. I've been on both sides of the table. And both experiences have given me some unique perspectives on the importance of a healthy relationship between roles. Here are a few words of encouragement for both.

Pastors, let's start with us. As we all know, an essential part of our calling is to spend time seeking God's direction for his church. This is called vision. Our job is to hear it, speak it, say it, sweat it, bleed it and lead it.

But let's be honest. Most of us aren't nearly as consistent or clear in casting vision as we should be. We need help. Which is part of the reason it's so important to surround ourselves with people who are passionate about clear and creative communication, aka the communications team! After all, a good communications team will help add feeling and emotion to the vision. They will help bring consistency and clarity, which in the end helps make the vision stickier. But pastors, don't forget, our communications teams need to be empowered and given permission to do this.

Now, let me talk to my communication friends. My number one word of advice to you is... be patient. As a pastor, I can tell you that sometimes it takes a while to gain clarity on where God is leading our hearts. While I think it's healthy to push for clarity, don't leave your patience at the door.

Same thing for us pastors. We need to be patient too. Remember, your communications team is probably more passionate (and definitely more anal) than you are about clear communication. They eat, breathe and sleep communication all the time, so they're bound to constantly push for clarity. Instead of being threatened by it, embrace it. Allow God to use it to clarify what He's speaking to your heart.

Secondly, communications team, ask a lot of questions! Remember, your job begins by understanding what God is doing in your pastor's heart. Stephen Covey says it well, "Seek first to understand, than to be understood." Great advice. Focus on asking questions that will help clarify the vision. And once you receive an answer, repeat it back! Put it in your own words and do whatever you need to do to gain clarity.

And pastors, let me encourage you to give your communication teams the time and space to ask questions. And I'm talking about your time. Communicating vision through multiple layers is risky. No, better yet, it's stupid. Remember the game telephone? God's vision for your church can't afford to be miscommunicated. Giving your communications team that time and space will not only help them gain clarity—but it will also provide you with a safe environment to practice saying it over and over, as well as identify effective words, phrases, illustrations and stories that connect with the hearts of people.

Pastors and communications teams, the bottom line is you need each other! Because when you have a leader who has received a compelling vision from God, and a communications team that is committed to creatively and consistently communicating it, you then have the ingredients for something beautiful! So let's close those gaps and work together in doing our part of bringing God's kingdom on earth as it is in heaven.

Scott Hodge is an artist, pastor, activist and writer. He leads The Orchard Community in Aurora, Ill.

Web: IAmScottHodge.com
Twitter: @ScottHodge

There are four types of tribal communication:

1. Leader to tribe member.
2. Tribe member to leader.
3. Tribe member to tribe member.
4. Tribe member to outsider.

We spend most of our energy in the church (and business) world on #1.

Think about it.

We get up on stage on Sunday and do #1. We send out eblasts and do #1. We write books and do #1. Then we upgrade to the latest craze and do a podcast (more of #1). And for kicks we send out a survey and think we're doing #2 well.

But the reality is that #3 and #4 are what change the world.

We used to think that the best person to reach an outsider was the leader of a tribe. It turns out that isn't true. The best person to reach an outsider is someone who has a relationship with them.

What would happen if we shifted our strategy to #3 and #4?

Jon Dale is the chief happiness officer and co-founder of Moolala. He's also a husband, father, adventurer and agent of change.

Web: JonDale.com
Twitter: @JonDale

Ministry leaders with a communication agenda have good intentions. They have real needs. They want to help people. They are ready to convince you that their next big ministry opportunity is worthy of top billing. And they are not alone. The line of people hoping to get the attention of the church is endless.

Communication is a powerful tool that can move people toward becoming an unstoppable force for good. This will not happen when all messages share equal importance. If every need is perceived as vital, all of them become less meaningful. This healthy tension between what *can be* communicated and what *must be* communicated is a good thing. Communication professionals exist to live in the tension between can and must. Pursuing the tension produces clarity. Refusing to embrace the tension blurs the message.

As communicators, our role is to define the message by pursuing the tension and encouraging our leaders to set priorities. Doing so narrows the focus to the essential and enables us to define a "yes!" Knowing what a "yes" looks like enables us to also know when to say "no." Define your "yes" by discovering what is unique about your church. Where is God using your church to bring transformation? What is the best way to tell that story?

There will always be plenty of ministry opportunities. Only a few should be shared. It's like sitting on a quarter horse ready to unleash its strength. If more than one person tries to control the reins, the horse will become confused and its strength can't be fully realized. Your pace will always be limited, and you will always be left wondering which direction you should be going. If you are feeling pulled in numerous directions, so will those with whom you communicate.

Who holds the reins of your communication? If the long line of people at your door has the reins, you have lost direction. It's never too late to begin taking the reins again. It is rarely done quickly, but over time you can move the church toward its predetermined destination. When the direction becomes clear and the reins are relaxed, the power of simple communication is unleashed.

The message loses effectiveness when the crowd controls communication. The church's voice is weakened, and few get the point. When the crowd is unleashed with a common message into the community, the collective voice will help produce an unstoppable force that transforms lives. All eyes are fixed on the future when the destination is clear.

Gerry True is the communication arts minister at Oak Hills Church in San Antonio, Texas. He's also a fast walker and talker who feeds his chocolate addiction and enjoys blogging, reading and leading.

Web: GerryTrue.com   **Twitter:** @GerryTrue

You're brought into a leadership position as a "new voice," with an "outside perspective," to "ask good questions" and "challenge the process."

You're screwed.

In this situation, there is a team of people you will join and lead. They probably will feel anxiety at your entrance. They may feel threatened. These folks might be angry at you before they even meet you. Your team might not want you to be there at all.

But all is not lost. First, no matter how much you've been told about the need for you to shake things up—resist. Be polite and observe everything. Ask a lot of questions, not in an indignant or belittling fashion, but as a curious newcomer wanting to learn from each about their role.

Meet with as many people as possible to hear their story and perspective. Take notes. Ask more questions. Show that you care for the people around you, that you're not looking to bust skulls or rattle cages, that you're an ally.

Find the center of the work. Memorize the vision and mission statements (but paraphrase them in meetings). Learn how the status quo flows in and through your team and others. Show yourself as diligent when given (or finding) your first projects.

Keep real humility coursing through your veins and conversations. Show yourself to be theocentric, rooted in the Bible and excited about Jesus. Share from previous roles in an openhanded fashion, clear that "those" ways might not work "here." Read widely and deeply and offer expert perspectives to the team so that it's not always your voice, but an outsider whose opinion may matter and apply.

Play your "newcomer" card early and often: "I'm new, but what if..." and "I might not understand, but could we..." Your ignorance of office politics also allows you to meet up a bit with whomever seems strategic, to help you get a lay of the land. Find out how you can build bridges to break through old, silly barriers. Befriend the people who have real influence with less regard for those who just have good titles. You have a honeymoon period that is valuable— invest it wisely.

And the team you lead might even start to follow you.

Adam Jeske regularly contributes to *Relevant* and is co-authoring a book with Christine Jeske on bringing lessons from the global church back to North America (IVP, November 2012). He serves as the associate director of communications for InterVarsity.

Web: ExecutingIdeas.com
Twitter: @AdamJeske

When I feel stuck in the mud and frustrated with lack of progress, here are five themes I revisit to see what I need to adjust in my efforts. Many times I find what's blocking the transformation in others—is me. And it's usually because I'm neglecting one of these areas:

Serve
The best leadership model is servant based—where authority doesn't come from outside sources but from an internal power. Transformational leadership doesn't come from title, position, tenure or finances—but from a moral authority that is expressed in a way of serving others.

Space
Give people the space to do what only they can do. Tell them what needs to be done and give them room to figure out how to do it. Sociologist and author Michael Lindsay said it this way: "You want to create a culture for innovation? Give people freedom and flexibility in their area and be willing to back up failures. If you don't—they will never try again."

Stupid
Many times people just don't know it's OK to have fun at work. Are you giving them permission to laugh, blow off some steam and get loud on occasion? Are you participating in the fun? One way to cultivate creativity and inspire productivity is to create outlets for diversion.

Stories
We tend to conform to the behavior of the people around us. We tell stories, we share stories and we are changed by stories. Positivity is contagious. At times, you need to forego the performance review

system, the rewards packages and the training programs and create experiences that get people talking.

Switch

Instead of trying to find answers to the question, "Why doesn't he get it?" or "Why won't she change?" the questions we should be asking are, "What hurdles are making it hard for people to do their job?" or "Do I have all the information to make a judgment here?" Switch your focus and seek the perspective of others. Switch your schedule and seek interactions that come with a different flow. If you're having a hard time getting people to buy into change, it probably has more to do with bad relational navigation than it does the change itself. Focus on the *who* more than the *how to* and the rest of the pieces will more easily fall into place.

Kem Meyer is the communications director at Granger Community Church. She's also an author, speaker, blogger and gadget-addict with a short attention span.

Web: KemMeyer.com
Twitter: @KemMeyer

Put your benchmarks against what God says is possible and not what man has achieved. Outside of spiritual growth and health, I consider that to be the most valuable principle in ministry.

Let me elaborate. In ministry, it is easy to look at how other churches do something rather than how the Bible literally models it. It is easy to look at what other churches are achieving and aim for that rather than what the Bible says is possible. Do not sell yourself short.

Start with the Bible
Take it literally. Model your ministry after its timeless principles. Only then look at other churches for inspiration on how to improve your church within its biblically defined parameters.

Listen to the Holy Spirit
If you keep getting ideas and nudges to do something unconventional, your decision to go with it should be based on if it aligns with God's Word and gives you peace. Do not brush it aside because no one else does it that way or because it seems just plain crazy.

Have Faith
It takes faith to pursue what God wants for you. The Bible is full of audacious stories that should not be possible, defy convention and seem just plain crazy:

- Building a boat for decades when you have never seen rain before takes faith. (Genesis 6-8)

- Lifting a stick to part a sea and create a pathway of dry ground takes faith. (Exodus 14)

- Leading 300 soldiers to fight an army of 135,000 takes faith. (Judges 7-8)

- Feeding 5,000 men with seven pieces of food takes faith. (John 6)

And then Jesus tells us, "The person who trusts me will not only do what I'm doing but even greater things, because I, on my way to the Father, am giving you the same work to do that I've been doing. You can count on it." (John 14:12, The Message)

So expect to do things that make people scratch their heads. Expect the glares, the laughs, and the title of "crazy." But also expect miraculous results that prove it is not by your work or ideas but by the power of God.

Put your benchmarks against what God says is possible. Trust in him, and do not lean on your own understanding.

Kent Shaffer blogs about church strategy at ChurchRelevance. com and leads Open Church, a global platform that enables church leaders to equip each other with ideas and resources.

Web: ChurchRelevance.com
Twitter: @KentShaffer

It's all well and good to connect with peers, to learn the best practices, to keep tabs on what's happening outside the church and to be on the bleeding edge.

But if our churches are to be the church, global and glorious, we need to remain connected to churches in hard places around the world. And sisters and brothers in such locales do not have websites. They do not send e-newsletters. They do not blog. And they certainly do not tweet.

Such people have a lot to teach us. Despite little or no formal theological training (though many would still benefit from that and we must work to that end), if you spend time with church leaders in the Democratic Republic of Congo, Laos or the favelas (shanty towns) in Brazil, you find fruits of the Spirit unlike anything we have seen within the United States. Most North Americans have rarely seen real patience, peace, kindness, gentleness or self-control, to say nothing of generosity, perseverance, prayer, faith or contentment no matter the circumstances.

God can use the perspective we gain from other followers of Jesus in crushing circumstances to balance our busyness, superficiality, addiction to novelty and self-centered faith. It's good for us to travel to hard places to further evangelism and church planting efforts and to alleviate suffering. How about some mutuality, where we just try to learn from our brothers and sisters? We're reminded all the time of how much churches around the world need us. Let us remember how much our churches need them.

Then we will be the church.

Adam Jeske regularly contributes to *Relevant* and is co-authoring a book with Christine Jeske on bringing lessons from the global church back to North America (IVP, November 2012). He serves as the associate director of communications for InterVarsity.

Web: ExecutingIdeas.com
Twitter: @AdamJeske

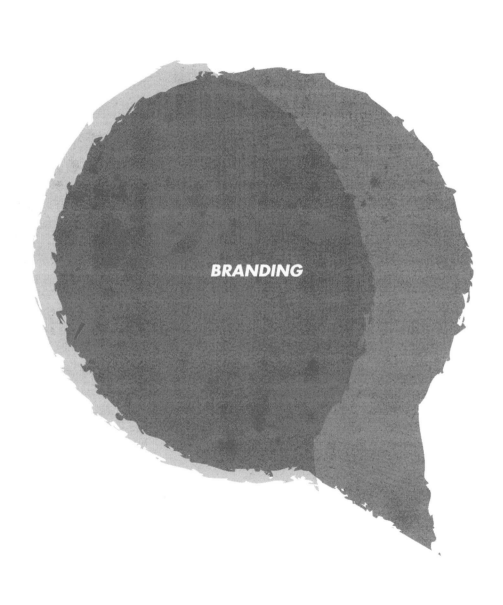

BRANDING

Authenticity and Your Brand Promise by Maurilio Amorim

Welcome to Your Brand by Charles Lee

Avoiding an Identity Crisis by Dawn Nicole Baldwin

Are You Intentionally Communicating Your Brand?
by Chad Cannon

"We are good at copying but not good at being authentic." Those were difficult words for a pastor to say, but both he and I knew they were true. As we talked, he told me he had visited enough congregations to know how churches freely "borrowed" others' identity. I ran into that problem early on in my marketing career as I was asked to create something that looked exactly like someone else's work. Even today, my company gets calls from churches that want to use one of our client's logos, brand identity and promises as their own. That's disaster waiting to happen.

I believe that's a problem way beyond churches and businesses. We often want to copy the style of something or someone without possessing any of the substance. I know church leaders go to great lengths to look and act like prominent Christian leaders without spending the time and discipline it takes to develop the skills that propel these successful men and women.

It takes more than plastic frame glasses, a shirt from the Buckle and an iPad to make you a good communicator, much less a good leader. Wearing a vest with a T-shirt and jeans doesn't make you any more relevant and authentic than wearing your underwear over spandex tights makes you a superhero. Substance, not style, ultimately wins.

Have you ever been taken in by the style but let down by the lack of substance? I'm sure you have. These are the times when an institution or a person promised something they never fully delivered. Sadly, many of us have walked away from churches, businesses, friendships and marriages because we fell in love with the promise of the packaging but couldn't live with the performance of the product. It's amazing when we get both, however.

When was the last time you walked away from a relationship or an institution because the product did not match the promise? What could have changed that?

Maurilio Amorim is the CEO of The A Group, a media, technology and branding firm in Brentwood, Tenn., and is an international man of mystery.

Web: MaurilioAmorim.com
Twitter: @Maurilio

Whether you acknowledge it or not, your church has a brand. The better question might be, "What kind of brand do you have?"

Your brand is embedded in everything that you communicate, facilitate and produce as a ministry. Your church's brand highlights the distinctiveness with which you embody your mission.

Your Brand Is *Not* Your Mission

In many churches, leaders often focus a significant amount of time (and rightly so) on its mission, vision and values. There's no doubt that this process is foundational to any organization. The problem arises when organizations take their findings straight to their multiple platforms of communication and development (e.g., websites, newsletters, programs, social media, design, etc.) while bypassing intentional strategy around their brand.

This usually results in unclear messaging, unrealistic perceptions and expectations (both inside and outside of the organization), and systemic inconsistency that will hinder development and growth.

Your mission communicates why you exist. Your brand is your organization's personality, identity and voice. It is not just a cool logo and tagline. Your brand encompasses the kinds of attributes you would want people to walk away with in describing your church after each point of contact with your ministry.

For example, Nike's slogan, "Just do it," doesn't necessarily communicate their company's mission to help athletes reach their human potential through their innovative products. Rather, their slogan communicates the kind of attitude with which they hope to inspire in the athletes who use their products.

Your Brand, Your Filter

Your church's brand is an internal filter through which you determine how you want to be known. Is your church like a friend you would invite over for the holidays? Does your church feel more like a professional acquaintance that you keep at arms length? If your church were a restaurant or grocery store, what kind would it be and why? How about a clothing store? Using metaphors like these help us to paint a clearer picture of who we are as organizations.

Your brand will ultimately impact your language, aesthetics, design, online presence, staffing and infrastructure.

A Practical Guide to Branding

1. (Re)engage your brand. Spend some time writing down your own perceptions of your church's brand attributes. In addition, ask both those who are close and distant to your ministry about how they perceive your brand. Be sure to compare the results as a leadership team.

2. Check for consistency in communication of your brand across multiple platforms. Do you sound and feel like the same church on your website as you do on Facebook or Twitter? How about your newsletters and/or e-mails? What does your gathering or workspace communicate?

3. Identify your main brand attributes (usually 3-5) and review them regularly with your leadership. Think of creative learning experiences that will reinforce the brand in the same way you do your mission. Your leaders are your key influencers of your brand so it is vital for them to be included in the process.

4. If budget allows, consider bringing in an outside voice that has experience in organizational brand development. View it as an investment and not merely a cost. Good branding will save you time and money in the long run.

Like anything else valuable in life, it will take time to develop a strong brand. I hope these introductory insights will give you some context and direction in your branding efforts.

Charles Lee is an ideation strategist, networker, and compassionary. He is the CEO of Ideation and launched the Idea Camp and the Ideation Conference.

Web: CharlesTLee.com
Twitter: @CharlesTLee

We've all heard the countless clichés about the 40-year old guy who suddenly has a mid-life crisis and begins doing all kinds of crazy things. Who he thought he was going to be and who he actually became didn't quite play out the way he planned. The scary thing is, this happens in our churches all of the time but it's the organization itself that's in conflict.

> Identity Crisis, n. "Confusion as to goals and priorities.
> An internal conflict of and search for identity"

So many churches I interact with are inspired by a handful of innovative churches that have captured the spotlight. But there's a problem when the inspiration of others is mirrored with pure duplication—stopping short of understanding the unique calling and purpose God has given to their church. This comparison game only leads to frustration and division within our church body combined with a lot of repetition that often isn't centered on our strengths. As my friend Mark Batterson frankly puts it: "We have begun replacing our own creativity and imagination with the imitation of others."

1 Corinthians 12:14 said the body is not made up of one part, but many. We can't all be the head or an arm and expect the kingdom to function as it was designed. So the question is, what "part" did God call *your* church to be?

When we were children and unable to fully define or articulate our values, we associated who we were with what we did. Growing up, friends saw me as the "artsy one" who drew cartoons and loved to write stories. On the flip side, my hand/eye coordination, speed and general athletic abilities were pretty pathetic. I was usually the last kid picked for teams, generating waves of sighs and groans by whichever team was lucky enough to "choose" me. Many years of consistent (but failed) attempts at any sort of sport that involved round objects confirmed I should not bank on athletic scholarships to pay for college.

Many of us believe our identity is found in the superficial characteristics defined by others. "The big church on the corner," or "The church with lots of missions programs." But if the building burns down or the youth program is done better by the new church down the street, we're left questioning who we are.

Our true identity is so often found at the crossroads of our strengths and our values. As we mature, we identify the things important to us that we're not willing to compromise. When lived out consistently, others begin to recognize us by our actions and expect the same in the future. I would never expect a vegan friend to share my love for a Ruth's Chris steak. Likewise, others have expectations of me because I'm a Christian and work with church leaders. When our decisions and our actions don't align with what we're known for and what we value, there's a disconnect. Knowing who you are (and more importantly, who you're not) is the key.

Dawn Nicole Baldwin is the founder of AspireOne and a senior partner in the mobile communications firm Jarbyco.

Web: DawnNicoleBaldwin.com
Twitter: @DawnNicole

To me, branding has become the "in" word as people talk about marketing and advertising these days, not only in business, but in the church as well. Branding isn't marketing, and marketing isn't advertising. Unfortunately, I believe this is a misunderstood concept because for too long we've been using these words interchangeably in our communication strategies. I'm going to focus on branding.

In your community, your church has a brand, whether you're intentional about it or not. As people interact with your church on different levels (driving by, walking through, marketing piece they get in the mail, community outreach efforts, etc.), an emotion is raised in them based on the brand that is being communicated. As a church, it's your personality, your identity that is being communicated, which is your brand. What emotion do you think is being communicated? "Crafting a winning marketing strategy is challenging enough even when you have articulated your brand promise and is probably impossible if you haven't," says Steve Manning, managing director at Igor, a branding and naming firm based in San Francisco.

"A brand creates an image in the mind of the consumer. It says something is different at your firm [church], something worth more than business [church] as usual. If your firm [church] is a commodity, your customers will choose you solely on the basis of price or getting something for free. If you've got a brand, you're selling a lifestyle and you can sell anything you want," Manning says.

At Outreach, we have to be very intentional about our brand, because we have seven different divisions that are underneath the Outreach umbrella. It's very easy for us to get away from the overall brand in our marketing and advertising. This is always a constant point of conversation in our communication efforts and we still have a long way to go, but we're getting there. It needs to be the same in your church as you think through the marketing and advertising of all of your church's ministries and events.

It's tough to tackle branding in 500 words or less. The goal I have for you after reading this is that you at least begin the conversation with your team about what you think your "brand" is and then to strategize the best way to be intentional about communicating your "brand." In some areas, just because you're a "church," you already have a negative brand perception in your community. This is why it's that much more important for churches to be intentional about their brand and the strategy of communicating and living out that brand.

As you can see, your brand is much bigger than your church logo, website, bulletins, programs, etc., which for too long is how people have thought of it.

Here are a few questions to start the dialog with your team:

- What brand is your church creating in your community?
- What is your brand communicating?
- How are you communicating your brand?
- What companies or churches that you know of are doing branding well? Why?

Chad Cannon is a marketing and branding industrialist. He's the vice president of sales at Outreach Inc., and the general manager for Outreach Speakers.

Twitter: @CCannon

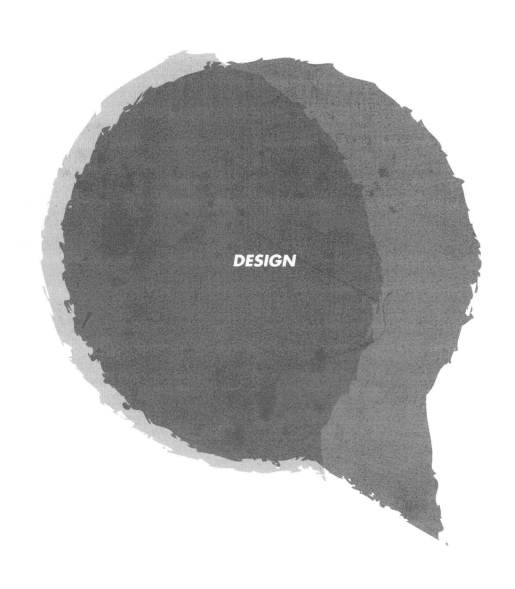

DESIGN

Everything Is Designed by Cameron Smith

Please Say Something by Michael Buckingham

Step Away from the Photoshop by Ben Arment

Presentation Is Everything by Evan McBroom

Whether you're a church of 100 or 10,000, having good visual representation will be key to how people will view your church. We live in a world that thrives on design. Look around you. Everything is designed. Product packaging, supermarket signs, advertising and that coupon jammed between the credit cards in your wallet. If you see it, it's been designed by someone.

With this in mind, the church has a responsibility to keep up with the rest of the world visually. This is not an easy task and there are churches who are struggling to get it right, but rest assured, there *is* hope! Let's look at some very practical tips that will help you, and your church, stay visually relevant.

1. Keep It Simple

Let's be honest, our nature as humans will often lead us down the road of over-complication. We need to avoid that road at all costs. In communication, there is a great temptation to give as much information as possible in one piece; don't be tempted. When it comes to design, less is more. White space is your friend. Keep it simple.

2. Know the Rules

There are some very basic fundamentals in the world of art and graphic design. You should learn and become familiar with terms like balance, composition, alignment, color, contrast and white space. The opportunity to cut corners and hurry through a design is always before us, but if we focus on the fundamentals and rules of design we will always have the opportunity to make a good design even better.

3. Start Small

Not every church can have it all when it comes to graphic design. Know what you can do, what you're capable of and do it well. If you're struggling to get things done, chances are you're trying to do too much. You can't have it all right away. Start small and build your way into multiple avenues of visual communication.

The church of Jesus Christ is the hope of the world. Let's do our very best to represent her with visuals that are eye catching, outstanding, meaningful and relevant. If you're struggling to get this right, just remember these key points: keep it simple, know the rules and start small.

Resources:
graphicdesignbasics.com/principles-of-design
digital-web.com/articles/principles_of_design

Cameron Smith is a visual ninja and creative catalyst working to advance the kingdom through graphic design.

Web: CameronSmithBlog.com
Twitter: @Cameron987

"Wow, that looks great."

In an art gallery, that's a well-deserved compliment. But while we are artists, we aren't working with paintings and we're not here to entertain. While my days are often filled talking to pastors about a new focus on the *how* of church and preaching, I'm asking you, the designer, to focus on the what.

Too often our projects look something like this:

In fact, we'd applaud a project that as an end result gives us a logo, sermon branding, visitor packet, etc., that looks good. But as The Mad Hatter said to Alice "You've lost your muchness." If your latest project only looks good, and doesn't say something, it becomes vapor.

Though we'd like to blame it on budgets and leadership, and while there are certainly times they don't make the climb easy, the fault lies in us skipping a step. It's the step of exploring and understanding the message of our art. It's creating a project that looks like this:

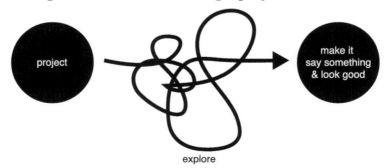

The purpose of the designer isn't to create beauty. Though, it will certainly be beautiful, our purpose is to help deliver a message in a way that delights and inspires. Like the painter, our work should be emotional, it should move people. But as designers, especially designers in the church, it must move past mere emotion and into actionable, concrete ideas.

And that starts with a pencil.

We must first spend time in an arena somewhat foreign to the creative brain that feasts on colors and imagery. We must spend time with information and research. We need to begin by asking questions: What are we trying to say? Why does it need to be said? Who are we saying it to? And on and on until we understand the objective of our communication. Layer after layer we begin to understand what we are trying to say and the people we are saying it to.

This is a time of exploration and discovery. The process of creating something beautiful, of saying something powerful, is not simple and easy but messy and complicated.

Once we've peeled back all those layers and we understand what it is that we need to say, then that pencil can do what that creative brain is aching to do and begin sketching real, meaningful, sustainable, sticky and emotional ways to say it

When we do, our craft inspires action and engagement, and it inspires people to listen and to change.

And that is beautiful.

Michael Buckingham is the founder of Holy Cow Creative, an agency that wants to make the church the most ridiculously creative place on the planet.

Web: HolyCowCreative.org
Twitter: @HolyCowCreative

Michael Buckingham

MTV calls us the producer generation because we've grown up creating our own websites, logos, videos and music. But your church—no matter how amazing it is—comes off as amateurish when you design the communications yourself.

It doesn't matter what the PC revolution has done to place publishing tools in your hands; you're no artist. That is, unless you really are an artist. And even then, you could benefit by using someone better than you.

I once attended an outdoor wedding where the father of the bride thought it would be a good idea to erect portable toilets around the lawn for the guests' convenience. Sure, it was affordable and easy, but the wedding looked like a construction site and stank like an outhouse. He didn't pass his idea through the filter of an artist.

All of us have a bit of that father of the bride inside us. There are moments when we're tempted to do it ourselves because it's faster, cheaper and more convenient. But if you believe in your church, use a professional. A great church deserves great art.

When you walk through the mall, you can tell the difference between the national franchises and the do-it-yourselfers. It's called quality. National brands "cloak" their ideas in a high-end presentation, where the store itself is an experience. Local stores, on the other hand, have blank walls, mediocre signage and standard merchandising equipment. But it doesn't have to be this way. Great design covers a multitude of sins.

Hiring a designer is not cheap. I have plenty of friends who refuse to make design a priority because of cost. But you don't need to design everything piece by piece. You only need a communications arsenal. Identify all the ways in which you'll communicate to your audience and hire a designer to frame those mediums.

When I plan the communications strategy for events, I ask a designer to create an arsenal of mediums for me to use. These include:

Logo / HTML e-mail skins / Website / Direct mail pieces Notebook / ID badges / Signage / Envelopes and stationery DVD packaging / Social media banners

Once these items are created, I don't need a designer on an ongoing basis. It's a one-time purchase. These mediums are all I need to communicate with my audience for an entire year. And I avoid any communication that isn't presented through these channels.

So don't do it.

Don't design your own communications. Don't settle for what's quick, convenient or affordable. Quality is the absence of non-quality cues. And whenever you try to play the designer, the probability of revealing non-quality cues goes through the roof.

I know you're excited about your church; but before you tell the world about it, before you let anyone interact with it, pass all of your communication through the hands of an artist. Step away from the Photoshop and ask a designer to give it a cloak of quality.

Ben Arment lives in Virginia Beach, Va., and founded the STORY conference and Dream Year and also wrote the book *Church in the Making.*

Web: BenArment.com
Twitter: @BenArment

Being sent back to the drawing board stinks. Presenting ideas, concepts and designs to your pastor and elders is likely part of the territory. Navigate it poorly and it's back to the drawing board... again and again.

Many church communicators feel outgunned at the presentation table as the dynamics of boss-employee or elder-employee complicate the presentation process. The first idea presented to leadership is really, really good—even great, but falls flat. The idea wasn't bad; the presentation was.

Here are straightforward steps to keep your idea moving toward implementation.

Prepare But Don't Polish

Don't expect your church leaders to see in their minds what you see in yours. Bring the idea to life with boards, images, sample copy and mock-ups. A stock photo and some sample copy go a long way toward making the idea clear and real for everyone.

Three-Minute Recap

Your audience has 27 other big projects fighting for attention in their heads. Don't expect them to remember all the details about this one. Even if they give you the "hurry up" vibe, swiftly recap goals, objectives, challenges and opportunities—all the background that puts the concept in context.

Enthusiasm Wins the Day

This is more important than anything else. Genuine enthusiasm is your most powerful presentation tool. Use it. After all, if you're bored with the idea, your leaders will be too.

Incorporate the Good Stuff

When feedback comes, incorporate the good that makes the idea even better and let it fuel the enthusiasm. Then, simply don't show enthusiasm for the less-than-helpful feedback. Let it fall away. If you do this, you'll find little need for discussion and debate.

Don't Seek Approval, State It

With all the confidence you can muster, lob a big, fat positive statement across the table like, "So, it sounds like if we incorporate your good additions (state them X, Y and Z), we're good to move ahead to meet the deadline in X days or weeks...right?" Watch for a nod and say, "thanks."

Shut Up and Get Out

After you say, "thanks," you're free to talk about the weather, the Cubs season or last weekend's big attendance numbers, but it's time to move on. The idea is now a project and it's time to get back to work and, thankfully, not back to the drawing board.

Evan McBroom is the creative director for Fishhook, a communications and creative service agency for the church.

Web: fishhook.us
Twitter: @EvanMcBroom

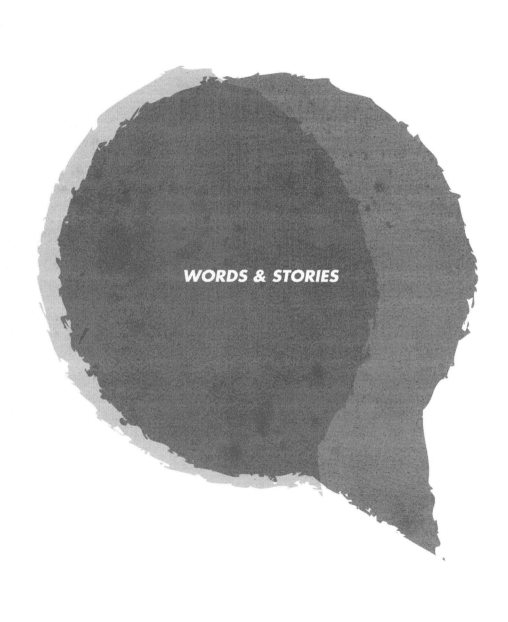

WORDS & STORIES

I think we are making a mistake with our stories. In some ways, this mistake goes against the fiber of what some people think story-telling is really about. But I think this one mistake causes us all to lose more readers and tell weaker stories than just about anything. Here's the mistake:

We don't leave any room in our stories for the readers.

Why is that a mistake?

What does that mean?

Simple: Sometimes as a storyteller, your job isn't to complete the story. Your job is to catalyze the story. You are the starting line, the jumping off point, the beginning. But you're not the end.

Why?

Because the best stories are the ones we tell ourselves.

The reason is that we each have our own internal language. I personally have 35 years of inner dialog I can draw on when you start a story for me. And I will write the ending with words and experiences that reach me in unique and engaging ways that no storyteller can access.

Take the beach. If you begin a story or a blog post about the beach and allow me to "write the ending in my head," do you know what I will write? I will write about how it felt to ride my bike to Crane's Beach, in Ipswich, Mass. We didn't have a lot of money then, my dad was painting houses to put himself through seminary, but we had the beach. On long fall days we would buy apples from a local farm and sit on the beach and look at the castle that overlooked the water—a gothic monster rising from the dunes and someone's imagination. The senior prom was held there and sometimes I'd wonder what that would be like, never knowing third grade would be my final year living on the North Shore of New England.

That's what I would write—but only if you left me enough room to tell my story in the middle of your story. If you pack it too full, if you put too much of yourself in your blog or your story, you won't leave any space for me, the reader.

Advertisers have known this for years. That's why the best luxury car ads are so minimal. They have a headline, a photo of the car and then white space. That photo and the headline serve as a catalyst. The white space? That's a canvas for you to finish the story.

My favorite ad ever did that. Here is the headline that sat next to a gleaming photo of a Range Rover:

"Not a, the."

With three words, they started a powerful story that tapped into all the built up feelings and emotions potential buyers have about what it means to own a Range Rover. This wasn't a Range Rover. This was *the* Range Rover.

This approach doesn't work for every blog or every story.

I write action, not art. (And we need the art stories just as much as we need the action stories.) I am more interested in the reaction to something I share than just the act of what I am sharing. So if you're a poet or an artist in a different way than I am, disregard this. If you write your blog or stories for catharsis, to get out what's inside, don't worry about leaving space. But if you want changed lives, if you want to engage someone with something more powerful than your own story, make sure you leave them room to tell their own.

Jon Acuff is the author of *Stuff Christians Like*. Prior to joining the Dave Ramsey team, he spent 12 years writing for brands like The Home Depot and Bose.

Web: StuffChristiansLike.net
Twitter: @JonAcuff

"But I can't write!"

If that's the first thing you said after you were put in charge of the church newsletter, asked to write brochure copy for the fall women's retreat or designated as the chair of the stewardship team, you're not alone. Many people feel intimidated when given a blank page and asked to create content. But when people say they can't write what they usually mean is that they don't write well the first time they write.

Here's a secret from a *New York Times* bestselling author—most professional writers, myself included, don't write our best on our first draft. That's why we rewrite. Getting something down on paper is the hardest part, but once you've gotten started, you can always improve it. Here are five tips to make your words sing.

1. Gather and organize the details.
What do you need to communicate? Most newspaper stories start with who, what, why, where, when and how in the first paragraph. Start by jotting down the information you need. If you're writing about an event, you need to know time, place and costs involved. If it is information concerning the financial status of your church, make sure you have the correct figures from a reliable source.

2. Write a bad first draft.
Once you have the details you need to try organizing them in a way that makes sense to you. For an event, start with the date, time and location so the information is easy to find. Then add more details. No one has to see your first draft but getting it down on paper it will make it easier to revise.

3. Beginning, middle, and end.

Does your piece tell a story? Even a letter needs an introduction before you get to the meaty details. To start your piece, have something that grabs the reader's attention. For a letter, you might want to try a question or a startling fact. For a longer piece, try starting with an anecdote. The middle should contain details or examples. Make sure the end wraps up the topic and adds a final punch.

4. Know your audience.

It's appropriate to use a bit of slang when you're writing the youth newsletter, but not when you're preparing financial documents for a bank. Be creative when you can but know when to be professional.

5. Get a second set of eyes.

After you've written and rewritten, chances are you no longer see the mistakes you're making. Ask someone else to read the piece for you. It doesn't have to be an editor. Even a smart reader can spot misspellings or missing commas.

Still having trouble? Find a volunteer or another staff member who likes to write. Many writers got their start writing for their church newsletter. But even if you outsource the writing, you still need to edit the final draft to make sure it fits your church's needs.

The truth is that anyone can write well, all it takes is a little rewriting.

Jennifer Schuchmann is a speaker, trainer and *New York Times* bestselling author.

Web: WordsToThinkAbout.com
Twitter: @Schuchmann

The written and spoken words in your church communicate just as much tone, if not more, as a flesh-and-bones human greeter on Sunday morning. We need to take a close look at both *what* we are writing/saying and *how* we're saying it.

Here's a question to wrestle with: Are you more concerned with getting your information out or getting a response? Care about the people you're communicating with. Go for the response. Take the extra time and effort to communicate in a way that elicits action.

One way that churches get trapped is by focusing on the organizational infrastructure instead of the felt-need values of the people. For example, is it more important that people know where they land on your pathway or that they know how to maintain forward momentum in their journey? No one is motivated when they feel like a tiny cog in a big machine. Instead of telling people how they fit in your church's grand plan, tell them how/why things will help them connect to and grow in Jesus.

Another communications misstep is using archaic and heavy language. It doesn't help people. In fact, it probably paralyzes most of them. You don't want to cut folks off at the knees before they even get the chance to engage with your church's culture (and, more importantly, Jesus). Make your communication fresh and light:

What is fresh?
- Current/contemporary
- Refreshing

What is light?
- Easy to understand
- Casual

I'm not suggesting that you dumb down your language. I'm suggesting that you make it approachable. You can keep it fresh and light while still communicating the deep value of what you're saying. If you care that much about your message, you need to care equally about how it is perceived.

It is worth your time and energy to break down complex concepts and methods into approachable, smaller bites. Why would you want to waste your time on writing things that don't call people to action? As a person in the communications field, this task should excite you! We have an incredible calling and role. God has chosen to use us and our gifts to help put today's culture in touch with his truth.

Let's make it happen.

Danielle Hartland is the communications director at Grace Church in McKean, Penn. Her goal is to create and foster communications strategies that cut *through* without cutting *in*.

Web: daniellehartland.posterous.com
Twitter: @DanielleSuzanne

In the morning, I usually walk through the old auditorium of our church on my way to get my daily dose of coffee. This is the place where I was fed for so many years as a believer. During times of powerful worship and challenging teaching I remember thinking, "It would be incredible to be a part of all of this." And now I am—as the web manager for Willow Creek Community Church. So when I walk through the old auditorium, I often pause in awe that God has called me here to do his work. Then, I suddenly remember I really need coffee to do that work.

I am blessed to have my job. Over the course of my career, I have been fortunate to have had interesting, fun work that has satisfied the overachieving, Type A personality in me. But, working at Willow Creek is different. The work is hard; the hours can be long. I experience restless nights when I wonder if I truly have what it takes. Wow, where was I going with this? Oh yes, but in the end, I know because God has called me to this place, I can rely on him for whatever strength I need to do what needs to be done. I rest assured in his calling.

What I do can truly make a difference in someone's life. I am not trying to be dramatic, but I believe God uses our work in ways we cannot possibly fathom.

Stories come in every day about what God is doing—work that he let me be a part of. Seed packs were sent to Africa, but only after people signed up online to pack them during our spring compassion initiative. A runner in Nebraska is thankful for a podcast so she can listen and be fed while she pounds the pavement on her morning run. Community and encouragement happens on our Facebook page on a daily basis. When I hear these stories I am thankful to have been a part of making it happen.

For every story I've heard, there are dozens I haven't, yet I know they are out there. The addict living without hope who finds our addiction program and reaches out to get the help he needs. The non-believer who walks through our door for the first time after Googling "local church" in a desperate hour. The single mom who signs up her kids for the workshop that will help them deal with a nasty divorce. The anonymous donation given online that brought hope to Haiti after an earthquake devastated the country. Or the person who finally found the bathroom after reading a map posted at one of our lobby kiosks.

I quietly celebrate these stories (maybe not that last one). They humble me; I am thankful for the work God does through them and I look forward to celebrating them in heaven. I can't believe that God has called me to this place and to these people. Where else could I combine my passion for the web and my love for God?

Now, time for more coffee.

K.C. Walsh is the manager of web and software development at Willow Creek Community Church.

Twitter: @KCWalsh24

We all like to think we're eloquent and witty wordsmiths. In moments, we might be. But wit and eloquence are overrated.

If stringing words together into glamorous, heartfelt and persuasive messages is only about creating catchy taglines, trendy ministry names, sexy message series titles and pithy vision statements, then the words are meaningless and the work is purposeles.

Eloquent or witty catchphrases may stop us in our tracks, make us stand in awe, laugh hilariously, or even move us to tears—but only momentarily.

Words must be tangible. They should compel us to care and prompt us to action. They're powerful and necessary tools. They should make us curious, and make us want more.

Words are like grandiose, ornately hand-carved mahogany double doors inviting us into a room... each line carved by a different tool... each concentric circle unlike the next... each familiar geometric shape remarkably elegant... each custom-made antique bronze hinge flawed, yet perfect... letters etched in arched and beveled glass showing the doors have meaning.

The doors pique our imagination, but what lies beyond makes them worthwhile.

Maybe the meticulousness that went into crafting the doors isn't reflected in the drab, boring, off-white room we found once we opened them. (The analogy: words are glamorous accessories, but lack substance.)

Maybe the doors are deceptively seductive. Merely a way of coaxing us into a damp, dingy, musty basement (reminiscent of a horror movie) that leaves us wondering about what is lurking behind the many cobwebs and inside the eerie closets. (The analogy: words are misleading because the expectations and experiences don't jive.)

But maybe we're instantly captivated by the room's beauty... arched ceilings, handcrafted woodwork, intricate paintings and stunning views. It's more than we imagined. We don't want to leave. We keep discovering new things. Then we look back to the doors and appreciate where they led us... so much so, that we can't wait to tell others about the amazing destination. (The analogy: words have become real and memorable experiences that move people to action.)

Words are only one-dimensional. We can't just say something. We need to show it. We need to prove it. We need to engage the senses. Create multi-dimensional experiences. Experiences communicate more than words ever can.

Great communicators don't just speak, write or design cool collateral. Great communicators breathe life into words, give words a heartbeat, and create an environment where words *live* inside of people.

Dawn Bryant is a communication-crazed Jesus follower who is overwhelmed by thankfulness for God's radical grace in her life. She's a lay pastor for Bloom Church in St. Paul, Minn.

Web: SimplicityTalks.com
Twitter: @SimplyDawnB

One of the most powerful tools any church has to reach people is a first-person story of a changed life.

"My life completely turned around."

"We filed for divorce, and now our marriage is completely restored."

"It happened to me, and it can happen to you" is the irresistible pull of a story with a happy ending, going back almost 2,000 years to "all I know is, I was blind but now I see."

In the amazing book by Daniel Taylor, *Tell Me a Story: The Life-Shaping Power of Our Stories*, the author explains, "We hunger for stories of all kinds, then, because we are busy trying to figure out the plot and theme of our own story and are eager for hints."

Taylor believes every story is essentially an invitation: "You come too." He gives an example: "Smokey the Bear was more effective in getting a generation of Americans to worry about forest fires than a lab full of scientists are in making us worry about global warming."

As believers, "You come too" is an introduction to the ultimate happy ending, with the assurance that mistakes along the way—even horrible ones—can be turned right. We see even the most mundane, uneventful lives infused with meaning because while in earthly disguise we labor in service to the king.

And the best part is, no matter what size church you have, telling stories doesn't require expensive equipment or complicated multimedia. You really need just one thing: People whose lives are being changed by the gospel message. Ask them for their stories. Ask in e-mails. Ask them to write their stories down. Ask them in person.

Then, tell those stories. Video them if you want. Print them (with permission). Let nervous people read their story from shaking notebook paper if they're willing—God bless 'em. Their courage will move others. The more you tell stories, the more people understand their value and want to share their own.

In the seats of our churches are people overwhelmed by conflict and discouraged by bad decisions. They want to believe there is still hope—that their own life story can still be meaningful. The gospel message incarnated in a personal story becomes an irresistible invitation: "You come too."

Jan Lynn is a freelance writer and communications director at Eastside Christian Church in Fullerton, Calif.

Web: TheViewFromHer.com
Twitter: @Jan_Lynn

Stories are at the root of every culture. They have the power to spark action, to transmit values, to share knowledge and to sell vision. Stories are the language of success and celebration—they bring about serious, positive change. Yet the art of storytelling is the most underrated tool in any organization.

The church is a storytelling machine. Narratives of changed lives, transformation, renewal and, most importantly, the gospel include every component of a great story. But we communicate it like a textbook rather than a story.

In many ways, story has taken a back seat to the cultural wave drowning out the unique voice of many churches. They have lost their brand and market place, instead creating fractured communication and presentation. Churches need greater content and less distraction in the stories they tell. We should revive the power of testimony to inspire people with our living God. Story needs to be an integral part of your organization's DNA in order to move forward.

Every church constantly tries recruiting volunteers. Our normal tactics were not working, in many ways just creating white noise. Pulling from experience, we created an internal campaign around a demographical cross-section of our people and how they found purpose in ministry at Lawton First.

This campaign used the power of story to inspire people not just to serve, but to grow spiritually and closer to God. One of the stories was from 15-year-old Cameron who had been at the church for seven years. He wanted to do more than come to church, so he signed up to serve in children's church. What he experienced was more than sharing the basic "Jesus Loves You" and "Do Good." He admits he thought he was just giving his time, but the kids were making a great impact on his life. His teenage experiences serving on Sunday mornings have changed his life forever. He realizes servanthood, a part of his spiritual health, allows him to actually be the hands and feet of Jesus. Cameron's story (as well as others') engaged, inspired and challenged so many that we had an influx of applications to work in our ministries. Storytelling helped strengthen our relationships with our people and with the world. Since that experience, we always look to engage with our people's stories to illustrate our powerful and loving God.

Jesus was a great communicator, in part because of the way he told stories. Through parables he reached into culture, telling memorable stories with humble imagery, each with a single message. His stories allowed him to connect to a wide variety of audiences. Though the church is limited by its rigorous Sunday-to-Sunday schedule, we are in desperate need of what C.S. Lewis showed us—how to combine great theology with great story. Communication and storytelling have evolved, but everything comes back to connectivity—heart to hope, Spirit to light. In the end, stories are cathartic. They add a level of authenticity and integrity. Stories are the way we connect.

Matt Knisely is a visual storyteller. He is the creative director for Fellowship Technologies and the co-founder of Good World Creative. Previously he was the director of communications at Lawton First in Lawton, Okla.

Web: MattKnisely.com
Twitter: @MattKnisely

Remember when adults would talk to Charlie Brown or any of his friends in the *Peanuts* cartoons? We never heard words, only the trombone-like "wah wah wah wah wah." Something is being said and Linus, Lucy and others can understand and are able to communicate with them, but to the average person [you and me] watching it all sounds like nonsense.

When people come to our churches and hear what we're saying or if they are reading something on our website or in print, do they have the same experience?

I don't know how or when it happened but we developed our own inside language. Our own secret code. Some people call it Christianese, but I like to think it's just like speaking in tongues.

We are saying some really important stuff, but all too often the message is lost in translation. We're saying things in a language people don't understand. We've taken something very simple and made it incredibly complicated and hard to understand.

Jesus didn't use words or phrases like justification by faith alone, double imputation, Ebenezer, transubstantiation, limited atonement, eschatology or predestination. He used everyday language, objects and experiences to communicate some of the most profound spiritual truths to his audience.

In our quest to study, understand and explain what it all means, we've complicated the message. And while it's great to sound smart and use big words, we're leaving people in the dark.

Language is often our first impression.

What do people really hear when they hear you speaking?

What impression do they get when they read your publications, website content or other printed communication? Are you building bridges or creating barriers with your words?

There can be a difference between life and death in the words we use. We have an immense responsibility to communicate the gospel with reverence for the message and respect for the audience that will be hearing it.

Choose your words carefully. Craft your messages with conviction. Are you bringing people closer to Christ or pushing them further away with the messages you convey?

People have limited time and a short attention span. Remember to embrace brevity. Give people what they need to know in an uncomplicated, easy-to-understand way.

Acronyms, individual ministry identities/brands and insider lingo can create tremendous hindrances for people trying to get connected. If something has to be explained or defined it needs to be renamed. Create easy on-ramps for people by clearly defining the path they need to take. Don't litter the pathway there with words and terminology that need to be defined.

In Acts 2 when the Holy Spirit came at Pentecost people started speaking in tongues. To the passersby, it sounded like a bunch of nonsense and people even thought they were drunk. Finally, Peter stood up and made sense out of the chaos and interpreted what was being said. In the end, thousands were added to the church.

As communications directors, we're not the people preaching, but we play a vital role in ensuring the messages our churches communicate are effectively and clearly communicating the message of the gospel in a way people can understand.

The throngs of people around the upper room in Acts 2 heard nonsense, but when Peter stood and communicated what was really being said, they came to faith in Christ.

We are interpreters. We're standing in the gap between what is being communicated and the audience that is going to hear what is said. We have a tremendous opportunity to ensure that message doesn't get lost in translation. Be an interpreter. Communicate with clarity and conviction. Do all you can to make sure your church isn't speaking in tongues so that people can hear the message of the gospel clearly and ultimately connect with Christ.

Tim Schraeder has over 10 years of experience leading communications in churches. He is a communications consultant and was previously the director of communications at Park Community Church in Chicago. He's also the instigator of this project and the co-director of the Center for Church Communication.

Web: TimSchraeder.com   **Twitter:** @TimSchraeder

There is a microchip in every adult brain. It is *amazing*. It helps you take your simple thoughts and cover them with smart-sounding language. You come out sounding smarter and more professional, but your message gets clouded and confusing. This is lame. It's natural, but it's lame. *Fight this tendency.*

Don't believe in the microchip? Think about the last time you sat down to write an e-mail to a client—or your boss (or even an article like this!). Most of us naturally try to write in a flowery, formal way when we sit down to write. The problem with this is two-fold:

1. You Become Less Clear

Using formal language, you tend to use more words. And you use bigger words. But in our Twitter/Facebook/sound-byte culture, attention spans are getting shorter. People simply don't want to (or don't have the time to) read much anymore. We now need to communicate in as few words as possible.

For example, flip through a magazine. Notice the ads that are most compelling are the ones with pictures. And the most compelling ads have very few words.

Notice how your brain tunes out ever so slightly when you see an ad that is mostly text—it's overwhelming. There's no way you're going to read all that!

Therefore: Fewer words = better. *Fight* the temptation to add more or bigger words. The longer and more complicated your communication is, the less clear you are, the fewer people understand you and the fewer people connect with you.

2. You Become Like the Man

We live in a post-advertising age. Most Americans have been so over-exposed to advertising that we're tired of it. We're tired of being sold stuff, and we don't trust ads.

As a result, most advertising is losing its effectiveness. Word of mouth has become the most coveted advertising channel, because we still trust our friends and we trust real people (way more than we trust web banners and commercials).

Therefore, using formal language lumps you in the same category as all those ads we're ignoring. We listen to friendly, informal language—it's our clue that you're probably not trying to sell us something (otherwise you'd sound more formal).

Not only will informal language connect you with your audience, by sounding more human, you will also distinguish yourself from your formal, stodgy competition. Lots of brands are using informal language to distinguish themselves. And it's working. Brands including Nike ("Just do it"), UPS ("We Heart Logistics") and Google ("Don't be evil").

In Conclusion

Minimize your use of formal language. Try to be informal wherever you can. Use conversational (even colloquial) tone and words to avoid sounding like the man. Try to sound like a normal person.

Also, minimize your word count. People don't read long stuff (this article is probably too long).

If you want to be heard, speak fewer words in a snappy, informal tone.

Jesse Phillips former web content manager and social media ninja for the Catalyst Conference. He is currently a freelance web programmer, wannabe entrepreneur, and casual tweeter.
Twitter: @JessePhillips

"Dad, I bet the Jedi are more powerful than God."

That was my five-year-old son, Elijah, after I tried talking to him about God. Elijah is into all the great stories and has a habit of mixing them up in his imagination. He wanted to know which mythical characters were the most powerful—Pokemon vs. Transformers, Spiderman fighting Superman, Hulk attacking the hordes of Bakugon (Japanese battle robots). Harry Potter and the Spiderwick Chronicles get all mashed up in his mind.

So we decided to communicate the story of Christ more intentionally. And that's when he made his statement about Jedi.

I lost it. I began a lengthy sermon on fictional stories versus reality when he interrupts again: "Yeah, I bet Star Wars could kill God."

I sent him to his room. Instead of going, he waved his arm at me, as if he was attempting to cast a spell. He looked shocked, as if something was wrong. His arm passed across his body again, and I realized he was actually trying to "force throw" me.

My wife and I would later discuss the incredible power of story. Our ability to communicate the biblical story in a way that captivates and inspires is essential in an age of rich imagery and epic story immersion.

My son was right to a degree. The narrative of Star Wars in terms of his faith did have the power to "kill God." The tale of the Jedi had inspired him and altered his behavior. He was being transformed into the image of Obi Won Kenobi. It had reshaped what he thought was possible and impossible. His basic matrix for understanding the world was affected.

We are in a story-saturated culture. People are wading through the plethora of stories desperately seeking meaning and direction from them. The gospel must be pronounced and made more high profile as more stories continue to be shared. Helping people see the ultimate story in the midst of these minor stories is one of the ways we can tackle this dilemma.

At least that's worked for my son.

Nathan Davis is the director of communications at Destiny Christian Center and the co-founder of Good World Creative.

Web: NathanDavis.squarespace.com
Twitter: @MediaPeople

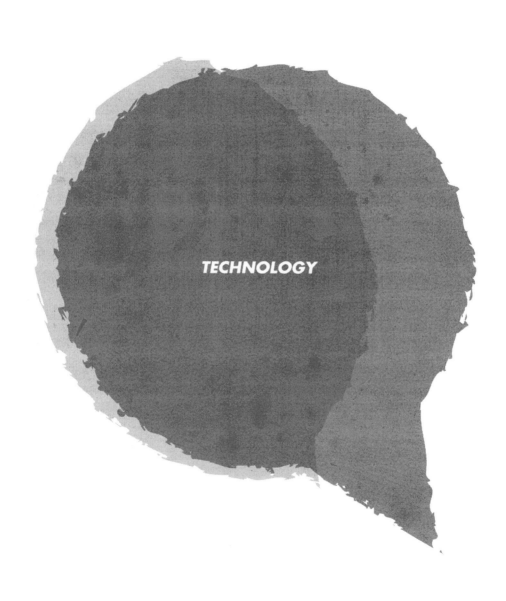

TECHNOLOGY

Growing up on the tail end of the Internet generation has been an interesting thing to experience. I can hardly remember our first family computer, one without an Internet connection. Since that time every computer I have owned has been connected to the Internet. Ever since the Internet became commonplace in households, it has changed the way we communicate.

For some more so than others the change may have been subtle, but regardless of who you are, I can almost guarantee that the Internet has changed the way you communicate. Even my 70-year-old grandmother uses e-mail to communicate. It is not unusual for parents and even grandparents to not only know what Facebook is but to have their own account.

So why do I bring this up? To let you know that I, of all people, am a huge advocate for Internet communication and marketing in the church. But it is easy to get caught focusing too much of your time and work on Internet communication, especially if you are from the generation that has been online all its life.

At a previous job, I spent a lot of time building and maintaining an online presence for a church. I figured out later that a large percentage of the congregation did not even go online regularly. There were some going online, but almost no one was going online to keep up with the church during the week (that's what a bulletin is for, right?).

So there are two principles to follow here:

1. Know Your Congregation

Don't waste large amounts of time on a medium that no one is using. If 90% of your congregation is not online then don't spend

70% of your time building your church's online presence. Don't even spend 40%...30%...20%... of your time building your online presence. But don't sacrifice the other 10% who are online. Just don't spend a majority of your time there.

2. Use Multiple Mediums
Communicate through as many mediums as possible. Go where people are. Use e-mail, paper bulletins, monthly mailers, Facebook, Twitter, your website, whatever it takes to communicate effectively. Although it would save some money to kill the bulletin, it may not be what is right for your context.

I know these two principles seem contradictory, but it is possible to achieve a good balance. It takes time, but it is possible.

Josh Burns is the director of web and social media at Park Community Church in Chicago

Web: JoshBurns.net
Twitter: @JBurno

The home furnishings retailer IKEA is brilliant in the billboard business. One of their billboards has their logo on it and shows three wooden stools with the simple tagline, "Come check out our stool samples."

What! They did not just say that. Oh, yes they did.

Shocking, intriguing, funny, effective. Perhaps more than anything, they gave us a quick clue into the culture of Ikea. It's playful, not pretentious. Self-effacing and alas... they have stools there.

The truth is, billboards have brief moments, even fractions of seconds to captivate and cultivate interest. To plant something memorable. To leave a mark. To spark a reaction.

How much time do you spend reading billboards as you make your way home from work? Maybe when you're on a road trip you might pay a little more attention as you roll down the highway looking for the next travel plaza to take care of some business, but most of the time, you're just passing by.

Your website needs to be your church's billboard.

Here are four ideas to give your website magical billboardesque qualities:

1. Keep it simple: Clean layout, engaging design, clear choices.

2. Say something about you: Are you conservative, young, urban, hipster or all of the above? Like your wardrobe, it should look the part.

3. Get to the point: The important stuff should rise to the top and look like it's important.

4. Point people to take action: Your website isn't the end of the line, it's the beginning. What should people do next?

Nobody is reading every page.

Nobody has time to read the fine print.

Nobody is spending hours on your website. That's what Facebook, Twitter and Google+ are for.

Your website needs to be a billboard. If people are only going to be there for a few seconds, leave a mark.

Jeremy Scheller is the director of communications, media and technology at The Sanctuary in Minneapolis. He runs a design business, provides running commentary on the Twitter and writes about his exploits in the kitchen at aknobofbutter.com.

Web: JeremyScheller.com **Twitter:** @JeremyScheller

It seems like microsites are becoming increasingly popular in ministry circles as a quick way to build some excitement. Creating these single-focused websites can be a great solution for your initiatives, but they can also be overkill. A few simple guidelines can help you evaluate your project's needs early on in the game.

Can you accomplish the project goal within your existing web presence?

If you've already poured the time and money into building a strong, versatile web presence, chances are that your existing site can more than meet the needs of your new project.

However, if your main ministry site just isn't there yet, a microsite might not be a bad idea. More importantly, this would be a good time to use that positive momentum to get the gears of change in motion for a revamp of your entire online strategy. Taking the time to build a strong web platform is a huge step in preparing for the future (and sadly, a step that far too many ministry organizations neglect).

What's the shelf-life/ROI?

Will the microsite be useful for an extended period of time, or is it just a one-off attempt to gain some attention? Will the expected result be worth the time and money to actually build it? Will your audience actually visit it? Do they have a reason to visit it more than once?

These are all important questions to consider, and their answers will help you chart the appropriate course forward.

Does it really need its own site?
This is what it all boils down to. Is a microsite really necessary, or are you just considering it for the "cool factor?" In my experience, our efforts are generally better spent pouring resources into some creative branding and marketing using existing channels.

Are you considering creating a one-page promo site for a new series? Focus instead on some compelling art and promote it like mad through your existing site, news feed, newsletters, bulletin, Facebook, Twitter and other viral media. Most ministries will find this to be a more successful approach in the long run.

Make Microsites Worth It
Microsites can be fantastic tools as long as they serve a specific purpose. Spend some extra time in the planning stages to make sure that they're "worth it" to your audience.

Eric Murrell serves as the interactive communications manager at Long Hollow Baptist Church and is the co-founder of MediaSalt.

Web: MediaSalt.com
Twitter: @EricMurrell

Eric Murrell

Doing web technology for, in and with the church is like riding a condemned rollercoaster. Flying down that hill is quite a rush, but when the brakes don't work it can get ugly. Once you start down that hill and momentum takes over, you make the mistake of blindly rejoicing. You're going to make it! You're king of the world!

A brief moment later the thundering coaster hits things like protocol, history and spiritual bureaucracy, and you're careening off the track. You're bruised and bitter, but the rush is still there and for some reason you get back on and try it again.

Too harsh? Perhaps. But here's the thing that I've learned recently that has fundamentally changed my perspective on developing software and leveraging technology for the church:

The two competing forces that exist are a tension to be managed and not a problem to be solved.

You see, although we want to move the church forward technologically (competing force #1) we also want to keep the values and richness of our history and culture intact (competing force #2). If this is a problem at all it's a good one to have!

I borrowed the "tension/problem" phraseology from Andy Stanley, pastor of North Point Community Church. He's made the point many times that in life and ministry, it's more about managing tensions than solving problems. That's where I uncomfortably-yet-comfortably sit with web technology and the church.

So how have I learned to manage this tension well? Two ways:

1. Be a Good Craftsman, Period

One of my good friends and business partners reminded me of a brilliant quote from Martin Luther who once said this of good craftsmanship:

> "The Christian shoemaker does his Christian duty not by putting little crosses on the shoes, but by making good shoes, because God is interested in good craftsmanship."

Although there's a bit of controversy about whether or not Luther actually said this, the point is well taken and I believe it 100%. You see, it is quite possible for two distinct elements of who I am to live quite comfortably together, that is being a Christ-follower and a competent and successful software developer. But I am not required to give up or necessarily compromise software development practices so that I can be a *good* Christian. My goal is to do well with the limited time, resources and gifts that I have, and that it will glorify God, even if I don't put John 3:16 in every other line of my code.

2. The Church Unique

Our challenge is not to re-invent software practices and technology for the church and then call it 'Christian.' But our challenge is to think critically about who the church really is—culturally, historically and contextually—and then craft a strategy that capitalizes on her core values, which (surprise!) are categorically different and unique. Our goal isn't financial reward but to reach people. The church couldn't be more different than the rest of the world!

What does this specifically mean then? It means that our challenge is not of men, machine, material or method but rather one of motivation. If we approach the technological service of the church as one that simply requires re-animation of the world's methods, a reconfiguring of existing models of engagement, or retrofitting a market-

John Saddington

place strategy, then we place the church as common, diluted, and poor. Ultimately we describe her as a "business."

But she is so much more, isn't she? Does not the church deserve more than that which we find everywhere? Then why do we not take the time and attention necessary to study the Scriptures (which most businesses do not do), prayerfully consider our rich history and then develop software and to use technology in such a way that is as unique as the church has always been? Let us not be known for a service of disservice for a most worthy bride and her coming groom.

It is my dream that a new class of Christian is born: One that appreciates the gifts of new technology without condemning the practices of old, who is able to marry those elements intimately with the teachings of Scripture, who executes strategically in the context and culture of our world, and who ultimately depends on the faithfulness of a God who sees the church as the ultimate hope of the world.

Then we'll be able to communicate the truth with excellence without over-spiritualizing our methods and present to the world a motivation that is as unique as the God we serve.

John Saddington is a blogger, creative web engineer and product evangelist. He loves WordPress, triple-tall Americanos and video games.

Web: John.do
Twitter: @TentBlogger

It's estimated that as many as 80% of people looking for a church start their search online.*

Typically it looks like this: A person starts by searching Google for churches in their community. They click through to the websites of those churches at the top of the search results. Based on the information and impressions given by those websites, they select which churches to visit in person.

What this means is:

1. If your church's website doesn't show up on the first page or two of the search results, people looking for a church will never see your website and thus never visit your church.
2. If people do visit your church's website but it gives a poor impression of your church, people will also never visit your church.

Don't misunderstand. This is not about competing with the other churches in your community. It's not about having the best search rankings or the coolest website.

I'm talking about loving the people in your community enough to make an effort to meet them where they are—searching Google. I'm talking about loving them enough to make them feel welcome once they get to your website. I'm talking about authentically communicating who you are as a church and what God is doing through you.

Here are seven ways your church can do that:

1. Optimize your website for search engines or hire a professional to do it.
2. Give your website a nice design. It doesn't have to be the coolest site in town, but it should be uncluttered, have a consistent color scheme and be easy to navigate.
3. Prominently feature a "New Visitor" section on your website.
4. Include a welcome message from your senior pastor— either a video or a picture and text welcome message.
5. Include pictures or video of your worship services and children's activities.
6. Answer all the questions you would want answered before you visit a church: How does one get there? What are the service times? What are services like? How do people dress? What do kids do?
7. Publish video, pictures and stories of what God is doing in your church: Stories from people in your church about how God has changed their lives, stories of how your church is impacting your community, and stories of how your church is changing the world through missions and giving.

When you love the people in your community enough to make them the priority on your website and authentically communicate the stories of what God is doing through you, people will be drawn to God and to your church through your website.

* christianitytoday.com/yc/2007/novdec/4.30.html

Paul Steinbrueck is founder and CEO of OurChurch.Com and the primary author of the Christian Web Trends blog.

Web: OurChurch.com
Twitter: @PaulSteinbrueck

Your ministry's online properties likely pride themselves at being an open forum where honest participation is welcome. It's here that people are real, thoughts are unfiltered and transparency is the golden rule. The open discussion these platforms provide is one of the best ministry tools at our disposal.

However, there are times when some form of moderation is a necessary precaution in our public conversations. When is the appropriate time to intervene? Here are some guidelines I've put into practice in our communities:

- Remove all advertising, unless it's appropriate. There's a time and a place to advertise your business or service. If someone in your community posts a question asking for a mechanic, it's OK to allow responses from mechanics within the church. However, advertising-related posts are inappropriate on something like a prayer wall ("Please pray that my house would sell. It's a beautiful lake view property that's just been reduced! Call 555-5555 if you feel led to purchase it!").

- Restrict duplicate postings to one conversation. Sometimes folks will be passionate about sharing their opinions and "fire bomb" every place imaginable with an identical post. Leave their comment on the most relevant post, and delete all of the duplicates. It's a good way to centralize the conversation.

- Genuine discussion is OK, even if it's negative. Your first reaction may be to delete negative comments, but if they're relevant and respectful, I think it's healthy to leave them up. Many times people may have a legitimate concern or a desire to have constructive dialog with the online community.

- Delete "drive-by" grudges. On the flip side, sometimes conversations can become unproductive (and even hateful), which is when it's time to step in and pull the plug. You'll likely run into folks with a bone to pick who merely want to blast out some negative remarks with no intention to discuss or interact (aka "drive-by" grudges). Those folks just want to stir the pot on an issue or cause controversy. Comments like this detract from the core gospel message of so many ministry efforts and are better off removed from the record.

Moderate your properties fairly and sparingly. Closed communication outlets are stuffy and feel artificial. Allow your social efforts to grow and flourish naturally—just keep a watchful eye out for the occasional weed.

Eric Murrell serves as the interactive communications manager at Long Hollow Baptist Church and is the co-founder of MediaSalt.

Web: MediaSalt.com
Twitter: @EricMurrell

Let's stop for a moment and ask, "What is technology, and why do we do it?"

To answer that question and really understand our social media and cell phones, we need to take a trip back to the garden in Genesis. It's there that we find the command God gave to Adam and Eve to "cultivate the garden." This is what theologians sometimes call the "culture mandate," and it means that we are in charge of taking the natural world that God made and transforming it into things that are meaningful for human life. This might not seem like a big deal, but if we skip ahead to the end of the story, Revelation tells us that when God remakes the world, he doesn't remake an empty garden. Instead he brings down a city from heaven full of all the stuff that humans created, like buildings, roads, trumpets and who knows what else. This means that "doing technology"—the cultural activity of using tools to transform God's creation for human ends—is a big part of the story of God and his people.

To find out how to do technology well, go back to the garden and ask yourself, "What was the first thing Adam did after he sinned?" The answer is that he invented something—clothing—by transforming the natural creation. And what was God's response to Adam's creation? God immediately gave him a free upgrade from leaves to leather.

Now Adam's invention served two purposes. First, his new clothes protected him from the harsh outside world, and God helped Adam do this even better. But Adam was also trying to overcome his spiritual problem: his nakedness before God. Here, his invention didn't do much to help. In fact, God's upgrade seems to say, "Your technology can do some real good, but I'm going to need blood to fix your bigger problems."

I think this little event tells us a lot about doing technology today. God encourages us to be inventive and to make new things, but at the same time he warns us not to put too much of our hope in technology. Our tools can do amazing things, and some of them might even show up in eternity. Yet they can't solve our deeper problems, and the redemption they offer is only temporary. So let's keep creating, building, making and doing technology, all the while remembering who's in charge of our final redemption.

John Dyer is a web developer for Dallas Theological Seminary. Previously, he's done work for Apple, Microsoft, Harley Davidson and the U.S. Government.

Web: j.hn
Twitter: @johndyer

My role as a digital strategist is to help companies, individuals and organizations develop sustainable internal and external goals to curate, engage and measure their online presence. In the past year I've stepped back at times to re-evaluate why I do what I do. The result of this process has led me to develop a basic primer on how stories from Scripture can help us understand the role of new media in the future of the church and how the two do not have to be awkward or uncomfortable.

It starts with a principle that I was taught over and over again by my pastor and mentor: The church is God's church.

The best place to start is with Scripture. Most of us might gravitate to the Great Commission, but for me, the best place to start the story is in Acts 1:8:

> "But you will receive power when the Holy Spirit has come upon you; and you shall be my witnesses both in Jerusalem, and in all Judea and Samaria, and even to the remotest part of the earth."

Keeping the context in mind, we find that Christ is talking to the disciples after the resurrection and just before the ascension. In their time, the "remotest part of the earth" might be Rome. We could draw a principle from this verse: "and even to the remotest part of the earth," and conclude that the fulfillment of the commandment is incomplete. There is a huge mission field for us today via the Internet.

The second part of the story comes from Paul's first letter to the Thessalonians. Paul and Silas had been beaten and put in prison in Philippi, released and run out of town. When they get to Thessaloniki they teach in the synagogues and a work is planted. However, they are run out of town again and head to Berea and then to Athens. It is in Athens that Paul sends for Silas and Timothy to come meet him in Corinth. When Silas and Timothy come to Paul in Corinth (Acts 18:5), the passage tells us that a change occurs in Paul and he begins "devoting himself completely to the word, solemnly testifying to the Jews that Jesus was the Christ." We have a parallel passage in 1 Thessalonians 3:5-7:

> "For this reason, when I could endure it no longer, I also sent to find out about your faith, for fear that the tempter might have tempted you, and our labor would be in vain. But now that Timothy has come to us from you, and has brought us good news of your faith and love, and that you always think kindly of us, longing to see us just as we also long to see you, for this reason, brethren, in all our distress and affliction we were comforted about you through your faith."

It is in verse 6 that "But now" is properly translated "Just now." It is *just now* that Timothy has returned with news of the faith of the Thessalonian church. This is the closest that Paul could get to an instant message!

Think about all the events and changes in technology that have occurred since Paul's missionary journeys. We've had Martin Luther nailing his 95 theses to the door of the church in Wittenberg. We could make a list of technologies:

- printing press
- newspapers
- photocopiers
- cameras
- video recorders
- VCR

- DVD
- television
- radio
- computers
- Internet
- telephone
- sound systems

I'm quite sure this is a short version of the list of tools available to the church. But let me share with you two stories of a church and a ministry that are using new media to reach the remotest parts with "just now" updates.

Last year I spoke with Kurt Ervin, multi-site strategist and online campus pastor for Central Christian Church in Las Vegas. I had originally set up a call to talk with him about online campus ministry and how Central was using the platform. He told me that one of the biggest goals of Central is planting churches. To keep in line with this goal the online campus had to connect them not only online, but offline as well. He noticed at one point that there were a large group of folks from a particular area in Southern California that participated regularly in the online services. Kurt and his team contacted this group of people by e-mail and invited them to join him and the Central Christian band for a special worship service at a local hotel. Out of this gathering came a small group ministry that has led to a church plant. Kurt and the whole body of believers at Central were able to experience the "just now" through the strategic use of technology. This rocked my brain! What a powerful story.

The second story I want to share with you is about a young man named Jake Bodine. I met Jake at Catalyst West last year. Jake is the founder of a prison ministry called God Behind Bars. Jake's vision was to partner with local churches and organizations to stream live high quality church services from some of America's premier churches to prisons all across America. The ministry gives prisoners the opportunity to create a life-changing plan by introducing them to God's radical grace, forgiveness and power to transform their lives. Prisoners have the opportunity to join recovery groups to help with the real addictions that these men and women struggle with daily. God Behind Bars provides a quality reentry program, completing the process of this road to freedom.

These two stories are just the start of examples of how we are able to experience the "just now" that Paul experienced. Our goal as God's church should be to use technology to plant churches, teach and continue to reach the remotest parts.

Jim Gray is account director at Beaconhill NW and senior curator of Threethirtypm.com He lives in the Pacific Northwest with his wife Sharon and three children.

Web: about.me/beaconhillnw
Twitter: @JimGrayOnline

People don't care about your website, but your content matters more than ever. I came to this realization in the midst of a surprising downturn in traffic to our newly redesigned website.

Shortly after they were introduced, we decided to take advantage of Facebook's revamped "Fan Pages." Our page was an immediate hit with our audience, gaining more than 800 fans in a matter of days. The momentum was tremendously exciting.

That excitement was quenched a few days later as I glanced at our analytics account. The stats for our main website were down for the first time in months. It wasn't a huge decrease, but it was a noticeable loss of visits and a little startling at first. That's when it hit me: Some folks just don't need our website any more.

An Unexpected Outcome
After inheriting the reins of our website years ago, one of my top priorities was to make our content widely available in a variety of formats. From RSS to podcasts, Twitter to widgets, if it has a geeky name we probably support it.

My efforts to syndicate our content definitely paid off, but in a different way than I initially expected. Any time we publish content, it's funneled right in front of our fans and followers along with everything their friends are doing. Our folks are better informed than ever without even visiting our website (and that's a good thing).

It's Not About Your Site's Popularity
Your website should be the best one-stop shop for all of your content, but not the only shop in town. Too often we focus on getting people to our sites instead of focusing on getting information to

our people. You're not selling ad space on your church's site (at least I hope you're not), so in the scheme of things your site's web traffic isn't all that important as long as people are getting the information they need.

But what if nobody wants your content?

Rethink What Matters to Your Visitors
From time to time, it's great to just throw everything out and re-evaluate what you really need to communicate. Ask yourself what information your congregation and visitors genuinely desire to receive from you, and build your site around that information. Once that's nailed down, develop a strategy for freeing up all of that great content into a convenient package that eliminates communication barriers.

Remember that your visitors aren't looking to be impressed by your awesome design, but to get information and connect with the church. Strive to make your website the best way for people to stay informed, but not the only way; there's a world of untapped potential online waiting just beyond your domain name.

Eric Murrell serves as the interactive communications manager at Long Hollow Baptist Church and is the co-founder of MediaSalt.

Web: MediaSalt.com
Twitter: @EricMurrell

Welcome to the future. What you are experiencing right now, with the rapid change around us, is a paradigm shift. The way we've been doing things will change. I know you thought the web was a new means of communication, but it's actually part of a greater transformation. What I mean is that what we are experiencing is rewriting the rules of how things operate. For example, we're seeing the transformation of the entire newspaper industry, not just a new way to read the news. Twitter, founded a few years ago in 2006, was part of the social media tools used in the regime changes in the Middle East. The sooner we as the church understand this, the better off we will be.

Be clear that the transformation is about much more than technology. Technology is only enabling the shift. Part of the reason these technological developments have such impact is because they coincide with a new worldview. How we see the world is changing. The late Peter Drucker worded it this way in his book, *Post-Capitalist Society*, published in 1993:

> "Every few hundred years in Western history, there occurs a sharp transformation... within a few short decades, society rearranges itself—its worldview; its basic values; its social and political structure; its arts; its key institutions... Fifty years later, there is a new world and the people born then cannot even imagine the world in which their grandparents lived and into which their own parents were born. We are currently living through just such a transformation."

We as church leaders need to think deeply about this transformation. The shift we all heard from modernity to postmodernity is accelerating as Gen X moves more into positions of power and influence. As a person involved in church planting, this shift means more churches are seeking to start new churches that gather primarily through small relationship connections (a term many use for this is 'missional community') rather than a large, central Sunday event. This means more people want to learn through experience and relationships while doing ministry rather than through one person teaching them about ministry. This will allow seminaries, churches and nonprofits who are not able to make the shift to connect with the shift in worldview.

You will experience the change more acutely in the years to come. But I have good news: There are many emerging leaders who already understand this and swim in these waters of change. That is good news because it means we don't have to put our hope in the current systems and structures around us. I have even better news: Our hope is in Christ alone, and Jesus promised he would build his church. Thankfully Christ will hold us through, even as things accelerate exponentially during this transformation. Welcome to a world where change will occur faster than ever and require that we stay connected to the one who never changes to guide us in this transformation.

Drew Goodmanson is the CEO of Monk Development and a pastor at Kaleo Church.

Web: Goodmanson.com
Twitter: @DGoodmanson

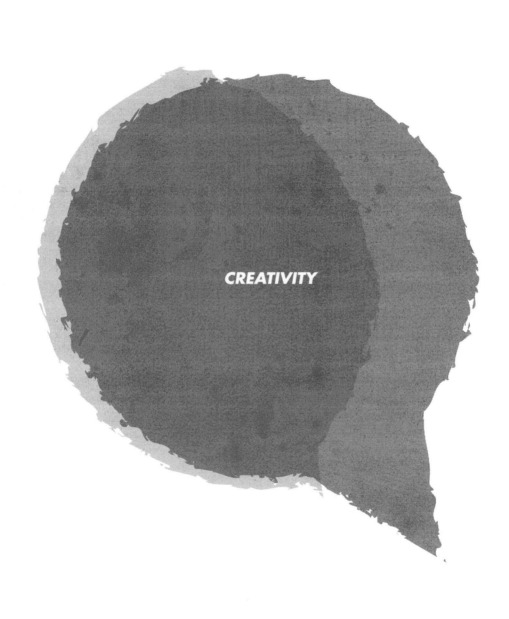

CREATIVITY

The Artist as the New Pastor by Blaine Hogan

Be Who You Is by Bianca Juarez-Olthoff

Creative People: Shake the Haters by Stephen Brewster

The Healthy Tension Between Church and Technology
by John Saddington

Sweet Tension: Creativity vs. Justice by Katie Strandlund

Moving Furniture by Corbyn Tyson

The Blue Duck by Jason Yarborough

Never Trust a Skinny Chef by Scott McClellan

There is a new kind of pastoring afoot. It is dynamic, ferociously creative and beautiful. This pastoring is happening in all corners of the globe, in fact. It evokes our deepest desires. It compels us to venture forth in search of true shalom, wholeness, redemption and restoration. It is truly a work of art.

The artistry I speak of is what you, reading this, are immersed in every single day.

You are a creator of beauty, a witness bearer and a pastor.

Every time you pick up a camera, a pen, a laptop or a notebook, it is beauty-making at its most basic. And through your beauty-making, you are becoming the new pastors of the 21st century.

As we move from our post-modern, post-Christian age of information and into one of inventive imagination, the artist is poised to paint a picture of breathtaking beauty.

If you believe this is true, I now pose a question: As we wait in eager expectation inventing new things, will you paint for us a picture that imagines and shepherds us into another way?

We are waiting.

In this age—also one of destruction and dehumanization—we are waiting for you, the artist, to show us your canvas. We are waiting for you to reveal the beauty that might be underneath the rubble of our neighborhoods, our relationships and our souls.

Unfortunately, many of us have given up; resigned to thinking our role is mere utility. More will continue to do so unless you claim your call to reveal the beauty in the broken places and raise your prophetic voice.

We are waiting.

We're waiting for you to call us into the deepest places of our soul. We are waiting for you to make staggering amounts of beauty that imagine another way.

For some to whom I speak, your beauty-making is already shining a light. It is crying out for us to believe that if he came once, he will come again. It is slowly knitting back together the broken bits of our story. Your beauty-making is connecting us—to one another and to God.

But for those who are still debating, I ask you:

Will you take up your call and step into the fullness of what it could be?

Will you help to cure our loneliness?

Will you dare to imagine another future and then tell us what you see?

> "To name something is to be somehow transcendent to it, not fully imprisoned by it, free of it in some way, even if, like Stalin, it has you under its yoke. To name something properly can be prophetic, a defiant act, an act of freedom. Indeed that is what prophets do. They don't foretell the future, they name the present properly—often times in a way that exposes its faithlessness and injustice." -Ronald Rolheiser

You have been the prophets; now you must be the priests as well.

You are the new pastor, and we are waiting for you to accept your calling.

Blaine Hogan is an artist, actor, writer and producer. He's the creative director at Willow Creek Community Church. He is also the author of *UNTITLED: Thoughts on the Creative Process*.

Web: BlaineHogan.com
Twitter: @BlaineHogan

"Be who you is, Bianca. Just be who you is." With a thick Hispanic accent, profound statements oozed from my father's lips. Constantly searching for the right words, he would encourage me to remember who I was, where I was from and where I was going. *Be who I is*, I thought to myself as an 11-year-old living in a city craving unique authenticity and the power of acceptance.

The simplicity of the statement was hard to embrace while intrinsically realizing I was different. I was the child who read for hours under my bed with a flashlight, wore thick glasses donning outdated thrift store attire, and ate beans and rice while church friends ate peas and carrots. Yes, while most children of the 90s discovered Nintendo and MC Hammer, I wrote screenplays and short stories about life in America. The America with apple pie, a four-door car and parents who spoke sans an accent.

I longed to be accepted and normal and, well—American.

As a child growing up in an artistic urban metropolis, creativity was homogenized and commodified into one culture, one language, one mold; a mold this 179-pound child couldn't fit in. So I changed—as we all do—to fit in and be found worthy of acceptance.

I consumed peas, carrots and apple pie. I laughed over words my father struggled to pronounce unlike the fathers on syndicated sitcoms. And since I was too legit to quit, I wore MC Hammer pants and danced like the girls in MTV videos.

I longed for originality but sought it by *emulating society* rather than *creating* from my history. Shamed, embarrassed, unsure, crippled by the fear of rejection, I compensated by neglecting my identity, history and culture. But running from identity is akin to running from your shadow; it follows wherever you go.

As creators, artists, storytellers and agents of change, we're designed to reflect the uniqueness of our creator. The acceptance we long for can only be found in the one who purposed our lives to reflect a divine plan.

By appropriating and embracing *self* into art, truly authentic and efficacious creativity births organic originality.

The beauty of acceptance frees the creator, artist, storyteller and change agent to design from inspired depths only known by The Creator, Master Artist, True Storyteller and Agent of Change.

I cling to my father's improper tenses and accented wisdom because I live in an artistic city still craving unique authenticity. Sadly, creative souls will continue to wander in search of what is truly authentic and divinely original.

Be who you is. See the beauty of brokenness. Embrace the power of forgiveness. Produce unique art *created* by history, rather than *emulating* society.

Be who you is. Just be who you is.

Bianca Juarez-Olthoff is a writer and speaker who is in love with two men: Jesus and her husband Matt. She spends most of her time as chief storyteller for The A21 Campaign, an organization to abolish human trafficking, but loves having dance parties in the living room with her two step-children, Ryen and Parker.
Web: InTheNameOfLove.org   **Twitter:** @BiancaOlthoff

You are creative. Why would you ever expect to be normal, average or accepted? Being unique and uniquely you is where your gift of creativity is hidden. Being different, out there, unique, uncommon is the very thing that has made you creative. It's your gift not your curse. People hate on the eccentric. Shake the haters.

You are creative. And being creative allows you to see different things. You hear different sounds. You feel the intangible. It's almost like creativity has become your sixth sense. Creativity provides you with a different perspective. You can't even imagine fitting in a box, or a cube, or a formula because that does not even make sense. So don't try. Shake the haters.

You are creative. Embrace your creativity. Embrace what makes you uniquely you. Embrace everything that makes you different than everyone else in the room. It may have been uncomfortable in your past, but God is going to use it as a badge for your future. Leverage being creative for good but never let it go to your head. Don't be different to be difficult. Stay true to the *real* you. If you imitate others then you have stopped being creative and started being a duplicate. You are original. Shake the haters.

You are creative. Be careful with your creativity. It is a gift but never allow that to become your identity. First you are a creation of the creator. Understand the humility of that gift. You have been chosen to reflect a side of God that most people cannot explain, a side that must be experienced. Never allow yourself to become a diva. Never allow your creativity to be a crutch. It is a gift and you are responsible to steward that gift with caution and care. Shake the haters.

You are creative. Use your perspective for good. Solve problems. Challenge systems and the status quo. Create experiences people have never had before. Tell the best stories anyone has heard. Then tell them again without words. Lead people on a journey toward the ultimate creator, because you are creative and you know the way. A way that most people can't see let alone navigate. Make the people, churches and organizations that employee you or use your skills better, because you see things other people miss. Shake the haters.

You are creative. So let's go! Let's unleash our creative energy. Let's change our churches, our communities and our culture. Let's lead and not follow. Let's push culture forward toward the creator and use creativity in ways that no one could imagine. This is our time. This is our season. We have been made for this moment in history. You are creative. Shake the haters.

Stephen Brewster is the creative arts pastor at Cross Point Community Church in Nashville, Tenn.

Web: StephenBrewster.me
Twitter: @B_rewster

Sometimes I look at the amount of time and money we invest in creative projects in our churches in comparison to the justice we fail to fight for and the love we fail to show and I want to abandon all of the creativity. I want to abandon branding, logos, well-designed print pieces and eye-catching visual media. There are moments when I look at all of it and so much of my heart says it's a waste of time and energy.

Right now you're probably thinking I'm crazy. And well, I would agree because that's about the time my other half chimes in and tells the first half it's crazy. I stop and remember why, as churches and individuals, we pour so much time and money into creative projects. God has called us to gather together as believers and that requires us to be able to effectively communicate with one another as well as with those who aren't part of our community.

For months I have been fighting this battle in my head and heart of which one is more important. I wanted a nice neat linear priority list. But every time I settled on one being most important it was only a matter of time before my decision no longer seemed right.

Then a light bulb went on and there was a wee bit of clarity. It's not an either/or situation, it's both/and. God commanded us to "go into all the world" and also encouraged us to "not give up meeting together." As much as we may want to make it an either/or situation I don't believe it is.

Perhaps we want it to be either/or, or we make it one because either/or is much easier than both/and. Working toward both/and requires us to live in tension. It means guarding the back door while also holding open the front one, and at times walking out of the front door altogether. And I'll be the first to admit that door juggling isn't easy. But then, living in tension isn't supposed to be easy—it's messy and uncomfortable. But I believe that it is something God calls us to, a challenge he gives his church.

Tension takes two; without both tension is lost. And without both I think we're failing to live out our calling as the church. Let's embrace the sweet tension between the time and energy we pour into our creative projects and the time and energy we invest into living out the love of Christ—the tension between gathering and scattering. Let's do both and do both well, not one at the expense of the other.

Katie Strandlund helps people get organized and put ideas into action through DirtyWork. She also loves creating environments for worship and dialoguing about art, faith, beauty and the church.

Web: CautiousCreative.com
Twitter: @KStrandlund

Creatives have an amazing innate ability to see things differently. They look through a different lens. See life from a different perspective. They really are no different than anyone else, they've just trained their brains to think differently, to not be satisfied with the status quo. They are most often the same people who were still coloring outside the lines all the way up to third grade; only to stop because then you were actually graded on being in the lines. Just like everyone else. And that's the problem with a lot of institutions and organizations. They have become a sham. A sham is defined as a replica. Perhaps it would be more fitting to say they're a black and white photocopy of the original.

When that happens an organization immediately becomes what I call discolored. We see life in color. We can see approximately 16.7 million colors. We think in color. We dream in color.

Now that we are no longer graded by coloring according to a color chart or by staying inside the lines, why in the world would we want to paint a picture of our life that looks jut like the one next to us? I love the scene in *Billy Madison* where Adam Sandler is coloring in class and Miss Lippy, the glue-eating, first grade teacher, walks up to Sandler's character, Billy Madison, and Sandler says "I colored the duck blue, because I've never seen a blue duck before." Creatives always live in that realm. They design things differently because they have never seen them done a certain way before.

Videographers constantly search for a new angle, a new shot simply because it's never been done before. Creatives are progressive. They can make all the difference in the image they create for your brand or in the material they are writing for your marketing piece.

Maybe you wouldn't consider yourself the "creative" type; but maybe you are creative and you just haven't seen it yet. I believe we are all creative because we are all created different and that is exactly what being creative is all about, right? Being different?

Then again, I have met and worked for the people who have failed to realize their ability to tap into the creative. They have the potential but they have been discolored for so long it's hard to break out. And you know what? That's perfectly acceptable. We need those people too. The ones who believe in the creative and cheer them on from the other side of the Mac. Businesses and especially churches need the type of leader who trusts and relies completely on their creative department to bring their vision to life. Life through story, presentation, imaging and implementation. The world needs more people like Miss Lippy.

Remember what she told Billy after he showed her the blue duck?

"Well, I think it's an excellent blue duck... congratulations Billy you passed the first grade." Pure encouragement.

If you are the Miss Lippy type, continue to motivate and encourage the creatives to keep progressing and keep doing things differently.

If you are the creative, keep coloring outside the lines.

Keep creating.

Jason Yarborough is the founder of ZapBoomPow, a communications consulting group dedicated to serving and developing churches social and digital strategy. Jason resides in Charlotte, N.C., with his wife, Donna.

Web: JasonYarborough.com   **Twitter:** @Yarby

I love the quote that is commonly used on the99percent.com:

"Genius is 1% inspiration and 99% perspiration."
-Thomas Edison

It may be a bit pretentious to admit genius, so I like this one from photographer Arnold Newman:

"Photography is 1% talent and 99% moving furniture."

The creative process is hard work. It's a lot easier to do things half-heartedly and buy stock video from Sermon Spice. It is very, very easy to rip other people's ideas off. I do it all the time. I started working in the creative industry 15 years ago and 1% of my ideas are halfway original.

When you work for a church the reality is that you have to put out a "paper" every week. It's difficult to create original art all of the time, especially when you have to design a really cool but respectful sign for a funeral that is happening that same afternoon. I have had that actual request.

But over time I have learned that when I pour everything I have into a project and I give my creative best, I am most satisfied. This happens in the 99% when I am "moving furniture." This is when the magic happens. The "moving furniture" phase of the creative process is all of the hard work leading up to that moment when you make a film, design a logo, paint a picture or create inspiring things.

Wouldn't it be great if creativity was something we could buy at the Apple Store? But it's not. It's moving furniture. When you spend time researching and learning the tools of your trade while everyone else buys stock art you are moving furniture. It is giving yourself to your craft no matter what others say. When you ignore the critics and hope that someone will be transformed by your art, even if no one tells you that it did change them, you moved furniture.

Every once in a great while you will get struck by lightning and good things will happen. During the other 99% our feet hurt, our backs ache and our ideas are challenged, but that is when you will feel most alive. You will have tapped into the creative muse on a level that can't be explained. In that moment you know that you are doing what you are made to do. It is in that 99% when your art is transformed into worship and becomes more than a glorified photo-copying job.

Corbyn Tyson is a creative director at the software company Monvee.

Web: CorbynTyson.com
Twitter: @Corbyn

I live by a simple credo: Never trust a skinny chef. It's a tad cliché, but it makes sense for two reasons. First, I want a chef who loves food, and you have to wonder if a skinny chef is really head over heels for culinary delights. (Note: As a lanky individual, I'm within my rights to make these kinds of generalizations.) Second, I want a chef who actively samples his product. In other words, if you're the guy responsible for making the queso, you need to try the queso— every batch, every day. And if that means you get a little soft around your midsection, well, that's a sacrifice I need you to make.

As the editor of a magazine, people often send me articles they've written. Some are good; some aren't. Lately, I've noticed a common thread among many of the bad articles. As I'm reading, I find myself thinking, "The author invested time into writing this, but did they invest any time into reading it?"

If I have to ask a question like that, I figure the answer is probably no. After all, if these authors read their articles, they would've noticed the missing words, the unanswered questions, the tedious tangents, the lack of structure.

I bring this up because I want to challenge you to try the queso.

Whatever creative work you're engaged in, take the time to consume it. Read your writing. Watch your films. Listen to your sermons. Browse your website. Navigate the church building using your signage. Subscribe to your e-mail newsletter.

Try the queso.

Yes, you're creating, and that's a beautiful thing. Keep doing that, but commit yourself to sampling the product so you know what you're serving.

In most communication models, there's a speaker and a listener or a sender and a receiver. At our churches, many of us are accustomed to playing the role of the speaker, the communicator. Let's do what we can to wear the other hat as often as possible. When we do, I bet we'll learn a lot about what's working, what's not and why. I bet we'll be inundated with ideas for new strategies, new channels and new messages. Frankly, that shouldn't come as much of a surprise—many of our best ideas come when we decide to listen.

Now bring on the queso.

Scott McClellan is the director of Echo Conference and the editor of Echo Hub.

Web: ScottLikes.com
Twitter: @ScottMcClellan

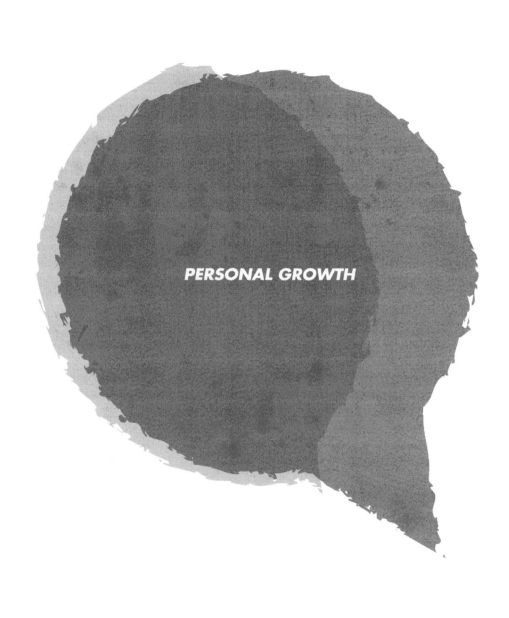

PERSONAL GROWTH

All Clear Communication Must Begin Here by Rhett Smith

Gutenberg Immigrants in a Google World by Leonard Sweet

Keeping Your Head Clear When Things Get Whacked by Kerry Bural

White Space by Denny Weinman

Narcissism, Social Media, Christianity and Me by Maurilio Amorim

Seeing a Revolution by Tony Steward

Communicating clearly is important because we live in a noisy world. Each and every message we write, send and speak is struggling for people's time, energy and attention. But the process of communicating begins with us, the speaker. It begins with the speaker being clear with who they are—maintaining a strong sense of self and identity. The speaker must communicate out of the knowledge of who they are, rather than what they can do or what others say about them.

In Mark 1:9-14 we get a clear glimpse of this in the life of Jesus. He is someone who knows who he is ("you are my son, with whom I am well pleased"), and because of that knowledge, he was then able to go out into the wilderness, resist temptation, and ultimately call disciples and proclaim the gospel. He communicated the gospel from the place of knowing who he was. He was clear about himself, therefore his message was clear as he proclaimed it to others.

Having a strong sense of self and identity is especially crucial in an online world where the constant chatter, validation, agreement and disagreement can distort our own understanding of who we are. If the speaker is not careful they can fall into several traps. In the marital therapy literature it's known as a "reflected sense of self"— when a person constructs an identity based on being in relationship with someone who will reflect back to them the qualities they want to see, rather than it being based on reality. In the techno-ecology literature it is known as the "saturated self" or the "mediated self"— when our identity is constructed out of mediated or external images, rather than emanating out of one's core sense of self.

What must a speaker do to communicate effectively? It begins with self-care and the act of placing boundaries in one's life. Boundaries tell us who we are and help us identify where we begin and end in relationship with others. Boundaries will look different for everyone, but it can simply begin by placing time limits on your use of technology; practicing social media Sabbaths; setting time aside for rest, reflection and solitude. Remember that when you set boundaries you are not only practicing self-care, but you are fostering the conditions by which you more clearly maintain your own sense of self and identity, which is the beginning of all clear and powerful communication.

Rhett Smith is a marriage and family therapist (LMFT) at Auxano Counseling in Plano, Texas, and author of *The Anxious Christian* (Moody, 2012).

Web: RhettSmith.com
Twitter: @Rhetter

"A charge to keep I have, a God to glorify" is how Charles Wesley put it in one of his more famous hymns; "to serve the present age, our calling to fulfill." To fulfill and be faithful to our calling, we need to be in a state of "here-ness" and faithful to the time and place and people to whom we have been divinely assigned. In the sovereignty and providence of God, we have been raised up, like the biblical Esther, "for just such a time as this." We have been entrusted with preserving the past. But we have also been entrusted with shaping the future, which only comes from feeling the texture of the times.

This "such-a-time" world has a right to expect certain things of disciples of Jesus. In fact, this Google world demands certain things of us, not the least of which is that we make sure the old, old story is new and hot... that we bring the promise home again.

The Bible says Noah was "a pious man... *in his generation*" (Genesis 6:9, italics mine). It is easy to be faithful or pious in another generation. Will the same be said of us—that we were devout not in another time but "in our generation?"

The problem with much "spirituality" making the rounds today? A lot of popular Christianity sounds like bad Buddhism or pseudo Islam to me. Christianity is not a vague, amorphous, ethereal religion; nor is Christianity a prescribed set of ritual practices, whether they be liturgical or litigious, religious or political. Try as hard as we can to get rid of flesh and blood and make Christianity into a religion of excarnation, Christianity is a religion of incarnation. It puts on flesh and blood and is inescapably material, physical, cultural. Christianity speaks in the locative case.

Some of the most successful websites are those promising to help you trace your ancestry and claim your ethnic pedigree. Everybody now claims an immigrant status from somewhere, and everybody loves to probe and parade their immigrant story. But when it comes to living as immigrants, that's another story. We're glad our ancestors did the immigrant thing so we can live off their sacrifice and glory. I was born BC (before cell phones). My kids were born AC (after cell phones). Martin Cooper invented the cell phone in 1973. My native culture is Gutenberg. I now find myself an immigrant in a Google world.

Sorry: It's our turn today to live as immigrants, Gutenberg immigrants in a Google world. Or to be more precise, *dies illa* immigrants, immigrants living in the last days of the past.

The problem is that we immigrants are acting like every group of immigrants have acted: When we find ourselves in a new world, what do we do? We circle the wagons and hide. We huddle in immigrant ghettos. We do everything we can to preserve the language and rituals of the old country. No wonder more and more of us are suffering from border syndromes: As people living with identities in both worlds, we are confused, uncertain, afraid, disoriented, on edge from the creaking sound of the shoehorn as it struggles to slide preconceived theses into resistant reality.

Christians may be fascinated with the future, but too many of us don't want to live in it.

Leonard Sweet is a professor, writer, preacher and thinker. He's been named one of the "50 Most Influential Christians in America."

Web: LeonardSweet.com
Twitter: @LenSweet

Once in a while, I find myself doubled over in a fetal position writhing in pain from the intensity, pressure and stress of building ministry and church brands. It's not pretty, but it's real.

On one occasion, we had a full team working overtime to renovate an 18-wheeler to tour the country for a national ministry initiative launch. The deadline pace was out of control. I was on top of the trailer, attempting to install mammoth vinyl graphics that could be seen from an airplane. Suddenly, a massive deluge hammered us and destroyed everything. It flushed precious time and financial resources.

In our line of work, a certain amount of insanity just comes with the territory. Like it or not, when you sign up for this deal, you've signed up for at least some chaos, panic and disorder. You know how it feels. You're rockin' along, getting things done . . . then *bam*! Out of nowhere, craziness smacks you in the face and things get whacked.

Here are a few ideas to help you avoid meltdown:

Reflect on why you do what you do and pray it through. Remember your passion for people and your calling to reach them. This will carry you when nothing else will. Sit, think and meditate on truth. Our creator is creative and he understands.

Look in the mirror. Assess and tweak your role. Invite others to tell you straight up if you are the source of the problem. Their answer may be painful, but at least you'll know where to start. When you do, you can contribute more intentionally and effectively. That's smart.

Revisit the original vision and calibrate your emotions. Occasionally, pull away and take a hard look at progress to ensure that your efforts are aligned with the original intent. This will help you focus on the end game. There's also a fine line between being emotionally committed and turning psycho-creative. Keep your emotions in check. People will like you more.

Talk it through and get it off your brain. There's no substitute for verbal processing. The more you talk it out, the more clarity kicks in. Clarity rules. Make it a habit to quickly sketch or write it out and make sense of it later. It's amazingly therapeutic.

Knock it out or walk away. Blow through as many projects as possible in rapid-fire succession. Work from the least to the most complex ones. If things get really intense, move to a different environment, take a deep breath and zoom out in your mind. Look at everything from God's much higher perspective. The fog will dissipate and your anxiety will fade.

Kerry Bural is principal of The Resonate Group and insane about helping ministries, churches and leaders gain momentum and enlarge their footprint through strategic thinking, branding and communications.

Web: ResonateOrDie.com **Twitter:** @KerryBural

Take a second and think about your schedule. If you work in a church, you are probably thinking about all of the meetings you have yet to attend, the projects left undone and the ministry hanging out there on the fringes. While the meetings have to happen, the projects have to get completed and ministry—above all—must be done, you have an obligation to your self. I like to call this obligation creative white space.

> "White space should not be considered merely 'blank' space. It is an important element of design which enables the objects in it to exist at all, the balance between positive (or non-white) and the use of negative spaces is key to aesthetic composition." (Wikipedia)

It's not all that difficult to see a need for balance. Burnout happens in churches too. If you're not taking a moment out of your week to feed yourself intellectually or spiritually then how are you going to be able to continue to produce at high levels?

Scripture talks about white space in Psalm 46:10: "Be still, and know that I am God." God has many attributes: God is omnipotent; God is healer; God is father. But more relevant to us here, God is creative and God is communicator. Now read that verse again as "Be still and know that I am creative" or "Be still and know that I am communicator" (speaking of God).

God desires for us to take a break out of our busy schedules and have some breathing room to create and communicate effectively. That looks different for each person. For some, it is 10 minutes in a day or an entire day to remove yourself from meetings, distractions, etc., and free yourself up to be inspired.

So what in your schedule needs to be deleted, shifted or boiled down so that you can begin to let yourself doodle, scribble, write, engage, read, observe or listen? Can you put it in a consistent spot or will it have to change each week?

That healthy white space comes from setting yourself apart with God as well. We're not going to be effective at our job as creator and communicator if we're not communicating with the one who started it all.

Denny Weinman is the assistant director of technical production at Sugar Creek Baptist Church, as well as a Twitter aficionado and creative geek.

Web: AudioJunky.net
Twitter: @AudioJunky

I knew I was in trouble even before I began reading a very thought-provoking post on social media by Mitch Joel, "Confessions of a Narcisist." The title alone was convicting. In his post, Joel unplugs from the Matrix long enough to see what we have often feared would happen: a feeding frenzy of the cult of *me*. Social media has empowered narcissism to a new level and given it legs to run amuck. He poignantly writes:

> "The true destination for most of our online endeavors really are the new media equivalent of the biblical statues that were presented as deities. These digital shrines that we create to ourselves."

The post hit a nerve with me. Intellectually I know that social or any type of media is inherently neutral. Unlike some who believe Facebook, Twitter and whatever new social network a 19-year-old starts tomorrow are the new paths to destruction, I realize they are just tools. They serve us; however, we feed them.

I think Mitch Joel is right. We are narcissistic. No, I am narcissistic. Too often my interaction with people is more about me than anyone else.

But what if those of us who claim to be Christ followers decided to redeem our social media footprint for a cause greater than the pursuit of fame?

That's the same question we should ask about the pursuit of riches, influence, knowledge or anything else in our lives. I've been fortunate to have known people who made millions so they could give away millions and people who are influential so they could speak for those without a voice. But am I pursuing an evergrowing online audience for their sake instead of mine? Are you?

If you have followed my blog for any length of time, you have read my diatribes on the pitfalls of bad strategy—or the lack thereof—in projects, businesses and churches. Some of us even have a sophisticated business strategy for our social media presence, but what about a faith one?

What kind of impact could Christians have if we were more interested in helping a world in pain than in how good we look to our digital friends? That's the question I'm wrestling with these days.

How can we redeem our online presence without becoming weird, obnoxious or confrontational?

Maurilio Amorim is the CEO of The A Group, a media, technology and branding firm in Brentwood, Tenn., and is an international man of mystery.

Web: MaurilioAmorim
Twitter: @Maurilio

We've seen amazing things in Egypt recently—the start of a true revolution. But the revolution didn't start because the leaders in the country provided a new direction, strategy or vision. Instead it was the people who finally spoke up, had a vision and weren't willing to back down until real change happened.

I see a lot of Christians online in the Western church talking about a renewal and a revolution—but usually in criticism of leaders and wondering when those leaders are going to get it. But until we are willing to own that vision enough to become the change the church needs, to speak up not just against, but what we are for, revolution won't happen. Those with this vision will have to lead the leaders to get there.

Passive criticism is powerless because it wants someone else to own the changes and it always backs down when confronted. Revolution can only happen when enough people own the vision of change, lead with a passionate voice and never back down when confronted.

If you want to see a communication revolution in your church, you can't sit on the sidelines and criticize.

Tony Steward is the pastor of technology and operations for LifeChurch.tv, a passionate cyclist, blogger and family man.

Web: TonySteward.me
Twitter: @TonySteward

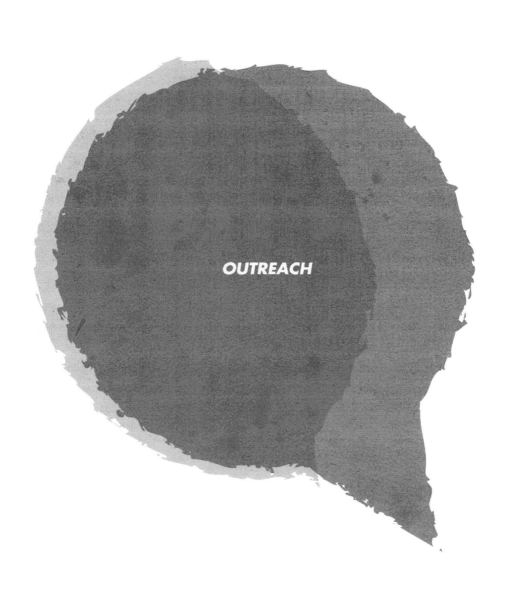

OUTREACH

Margaret felt imprisoned in a state of high anxiety. Standing in the middle of a large, busy railway station she was overwhelmed and disorientated by the sheer size and complexity of the place. She was running very late for a serious hospital procedure. She had never been to the hospital and was confused about which train she needed to catch.

A passing commuter noticed her high anxiety and emotional state and asked if he could help her. Normally she wouldn't interact with strangers, but at that moment she poured out to him the turmoil that was going on inside of her and where she needed to be. The commuter reassured her and calmed her down by offering to help her get there.

Like any commuter in a hurry he could have just given her directions to help find her train. But he walked with her to the platform where she needed to go. He waited until she was on the train and left. While they were waiting the commuter chatted with Margaret, which also helped to ease her frayed nerves. On the train, Margaret marveled at the kindness of the stranger.

I was the pastor on duty when Margaret's call came through. She called to thank the man and my church. She had forgotten the name of the commuter but was so impressed by his kindness and availability throughout that tough moment. She said that he had told her that he came to Crossway and that he had invited her to come along. She said our church could be proud of him and that is what church people should be like. I prayed for Margaret over the phone and again invited her to church.

As I put down the phone I was reminded again that just like what the commuter did, everything we say, everything we do, everything we are—is marketing our church. Every act of compassion. Every incident of sex abuse. Every act of love. Every abuse of power. Every act of kindness. Every loss of temper. Every cent raised for a good cause.

We can have the best websites, brochures, lattes, social media, videos, first impressions ministries—but if we don't have people like this commuter who authentically live out who we aim to be as a church—we've got nothing but an empty promise.

Steve Fogg is the communications guy at Crossway Church in Australia.

Web: SteveFogg.typepad.com
Twitter: @SteveFogg

It is common knowledge that a large portion of communication happens through body language. If the church is the body of Christ, what is our body language toward our communities?

We've all heard the message that the church should be externally focused and action-oriented, and many of us are out there doing things. Unfortunately, there are too many stories about us well-meaning Christians painting a building, cleaning a park and feeling good about it, all while leaving the supposed beneficiaries in a condescended state. I have certainly been there and done that. We must think differently to avoid this paradoxical result.

Could it be that our underlying motivation is our "body language"—the driving factor in the interpretation and outcome of our actions? Truly loving our neighbors is nearly impossible if we are simply doing things because "we should" or because "that is the role of the church."

To discover the real needs of our community we've got to go into the trenches. We cannot speculate from the comfortable church perch or expect speakers or whitepapers to direct us. We need firsthand experience, intentionally exposing our hearts and minds to new settings and contexts. We should be dialoguing with the homeless, interacting with the diversity around us, and inviting new types of people into our lives and homes. As we do this, we should prepare to deconstruct our own stereotypes and long-held assumptions that have separated us from a truly empathic view of our neighbors. We should also be wary of "completing sentences," taking care not to claim to understand people's needs without deeply knowing them.

Truly listening to people is the most critical—and hardest—part. As

Christians, we've been taught that we should be on the speaking side: sharing the gospel. However, if we are ever to do this, we must first have a listening posture. So when we think we've heard enough, perhaps we could turn the other ear?

After all, in the noise and busyness of our modern lives, who among us has spent hours on end exploring someone else's story? How about the life of a stranger who we may believe we have little in common with?

Of course, just hearing new information is not the end itself.

Ultimately, we must allow God to be changing our hearts: We must be broken at the depth of the needs of those around us. When this happens, we will shift from checking off good deeds on our spiritual to-do list to having neighbor-loving actions that are patient, enduring, authentic and needed.

Dave Blanchard is the founder and president of Praxis, a mentorship-driven accelerator program for social entrepreneurs and innovators compelled by their faith to advance the common good.

Twitter: @Dave_Blanchard

I've become obsessed with the kimono. That traditional Japanese garment worn by both men and women that the Chinese also lay claim to. Regardless of its origins, the kimono has been on my mind lately.

Here's why.

Hudson Taylor was an American missionary to China in the late 19th century. Taylor was a guy who thought and lived differently. Taylor wasn't your average missionary. He didn't just want to go and tell the gospel story to a group of people; he wanted to embody the life of Jesus in front of China.

This desire led Taylor to shun the standard Western garb he came over with in favor of donning the suit-and-tie of the Chinese world: the kimono.

Boom.

In one move, Taylor gained more cultural credibility than 100 years worth of preaching ever could. To the Chinese people, he became "one of us."

Taylor was smart. He knew that to be accepted into the culture—the very culture he was attempting to reach—he needed to speak the same language. By adopting the kimono instead of stubbornly holding onto his Western wardrobe, Taylor communicated, "I am here to share a message with you, but I'm also here to learn. I want this to be a two-way street. You can trust me."

That kimono got Taylor into places he couldn't have dreamed of, all for the sake of the gospel. The sheer audacity of a white, Western man wearing a piece of clothing reserved only for those on the "inside" was enough to gain an audience with even the most skeptical person in all of China. It was simple, it was absurd and it got people to ask questions. Genius.

We need to be more like Hudson Taylor. We need to look around and find the kimonos of our culture and start wearing them. We may not want to change the way that we do things. We may not want to change the way that we've always looked. I'm sure Hudson Taylor never said to himself, "Boy, these flowing silk robes sure make me look manly!" But we do it because of what it communicates to the people around us.

For instance, my kimonos are mostly digital. Having a Facebook profile is a kimono. Blogging about my issues with Fred Phelps is a kimono. Tweeting about my excitement over my new home brewing kit is a kimono. These are simple (140 characters or less!), absurd ("Picketing again? Really?"), and they get people to ask questions ("I thought the Bible said Christians couldn't drink?").

Wearing kimonos isn't for shock value or novelty's sake. It's to show humility to a watching, waiting, weary world. A humility that says, "I want to tell you about someone who can change your life. I also want to see who you are, what makes you tick. Hopefully I can share the same. I'm not here to speak at you, I'm here to share my life with you."

Justin Wise is a blogger, communicator and thinker. Justin is the social media director at Monk Development and co-director of the Center for Church Communication. He lives in West Des Moines, Iowa, with his wife, Kerry, and son, Finnegan.

Web: JustinWise.net   **Twitter:** @JustinWise

There is a lot of energy and a lot of resources in the church directed at delivering content on the web: blogs, social media, music, art, short film and on and on. The people who are crafting this content are passionate and gifted at what they do and as a result we are seeing some full on movements started on the web. Movements built by extremely talented creatives with magnetic personalities. Great, right?

I think we're failing.

I believe the church as a whole is going down the path of least resistance rather than taking the hard road that will lead to much more fruit. There is a leak in the pipeline delivering content from the church to the culture. We have this amazingly powerful medium of the Internet but we are playing the same game we did in the days of mainstream media. We think we are creating content that is targeted at our culture; the irreligious, un-churched, seekers, pre-Christian or whatever hot new label we're using, but the reality is that this content is primarily being consumed by Christians.

We do this for a lot of reasons but I'll just bring up two here, because these two can be fixed now within each and every one of us that creates content.

1. We value being heard above being effective.
A web initiative is launched and it gains an early adopter audience of Christians and from then on we craft content to speak to the audience at hand—Christians. Once we have a following, we want to keep and grow that following. It's not intentional, it's just human nature to do what is easiest. I have to forget my pride and stop trying to build my own little fiefdom, roll up my sleeves, craft some solid content and get it to the people that need it most. Rinse. Repeat.

2. We aren't having a two-way conversation.

Sure, we're comfortable talking about the latest gadget, musician or Internet meme with just about anyone, Christian or not. What we're bad at is having an honest two-way discussion of spiritual things. When it comes to spiritual content we shift into broadcast mode rather than meeting on a level playing field.

You don't have a relationship with a person online until you mutually consume each other's content. If all I'm doing is rallying around the latest 'web famous' Christian community, rather than listening to the people I need to be connecting with, I'm going to make myself that much more irrelevant.

There is a laundry list of things that are causing us to miss the target on this one. But for now you and I can concentrate on these two, starting with our personal content creation and delivery. Because after all, isn't this the whole point?

Vince Marotte is the Internet campus pastor at Gateway Church in Austin, Texas, and is the author of *Context & Voice.*

Web: VinceMarotte.com
Twitter: @M_Vince

The Christian faith continues to take a beating. The church has tried desperately to be "relevant," and yet we find today our perception is at an all time low.

Corporate giants like Apple, Nike and Starbucks have built powerful brands that tell persuasive stories about their products. But the truth is it was Christianity that virtually invented the principles we now call "branding." But today, Christians are rapidly losing our ability to share our story in a compelling way.

Dorothy Sayers was one of the famous "Inklings"—the writers at Oxford that included C.S. Lewis and J.R.R. Tolkien. In her book, *Letters to the Diminished Church*, she writes:

> "First, I believe it to be a grave mistake to present Christianity as something charming with no offense to it. Seeing that Christ went about the world giving the most violent offense to all kinds of people, it would seem absurd to expect that the doctrine of his person can be so presented as to offend nobody. We cannot blink at the fact that gentle Jesus, meek and mild, was so stiff in his opinions and so inflammatory in his language that he was thrown out of church, stoned, hunted from place to place, and finally gibbeted as a firebrand and a public danger."

In our present day efforts not to offend, I wonder if we're losing what actually should make us distinctive. Granted, most of the people Jesus offended were the religious folks. When Jesus was confronted by sinners or the suffering, he was far more tender and gracious. He saved his most fiery volleys for the hypocritical types within the church. Also, understand that when I talk about offending, I don't mean for wacky reasons. No one should be stupid in their presentation of the Christian faith.

But today, we often position Christianity as just another "lifestyle choice" and not the raging fire that transformed the Western world.

In our well-intentioned desire to embrace the culture, are we losing the very heart of the greatest story ever told? Are we trying so hard to be hip and contemporary that we've lost sight of the fact that the Christian faith is compelling, not because it's nice, cool or positive, but simply because it's true?

If we really believed that, I think it would dramatically change the way we present the Christian message.

Phil Cooke is a writer, filmmaker and media consultant. He's the founder and creative director of Cooke Pictures and a partner in TWC Films.

Web: PhilCooke.com
Twitter: @PhilCooke

What do you find when you type a church name into a search engine? You'd probably find the church website. You might find something about the senior pastor—his bio, his media ministry and/or his blog. For a majority of churches, that's probably all you'd find.

On the whole, I sense that there's not much communicating about the church happening online, outside of the walls of the typical church. Does that mean the church isn't worth talking about?

Sure there are lots of conversations online about celebrities, technology and politics. And there are a lot of people who are searching for God. One report estimates that 1 in 1,000 web searches is looking for information about God.

Does the church have so little to say about the God that the church professes to worship?

Yes, it's great to see some churches investing resources and hiring professional staff to make their church's communication excellent, clear and focused. But wait. There's more.

The Internet enables anyone and everyone to have a voice to communicate online using a plethora of social media apps. It's becoming common for the senior pastor and some church staff leaders to communicate more online than in the traditional offline, in-person gatherings and meetings at church. But their voices aren't the only voices of the church. The voice of the whole church seems rather muted.

As church leaders, we say that the church is not the building. We say that the church is not the organization. We say that the church is the people who are in community with one another—that is really the church. And yet, by and large, the people's voices aren't seen and heard online? Something doesn't seem right with that picture. Or, shall I say, something seems to be missing.

I'd like to suggest that there's so much more to be done in church communication. What if the church's staff and leaders' role was more about equipping and empowering the voices of the whole church to communicate—to tell the story of God's work in their lives? Remember how Ephesians 4 exhorts church leaders to equip the church to do the work of ministry. That work includes communication.

In the past, churches had classes and seminars to teach people to write their "elevator pitch" testimony. Now in the digital age, the means of communication is texting, tweeting, Facebooking, blogging and YouTubing. As the whole church is equipped and encouraged to continually tell their life with God as it unfolds in real time, these words of Jesus Christ take on a whole new dimension: "You will be my witnesses..." (Acts 1:8)

DJ Chuang is at the crossroads of leadership, new media and the church. He currently works with *Worship Leader Magazine*.

Web: DJChuang.com
Twitter: @DJChuang

The other day I started thinking about the constraints that we have as churches given today's current economic conditions. With that in mind, I began to brainstorm ways we can continue to improve how we communicate with the people we are trying to reach without spending any money. These are solutions that any church of any shape and size should be able to engage.

1. Improve guest services on Sunday mornings.

Stress that Sunday mornings are a time for your hospitality team to be focused on visitors. The number one reason people will come back to your church is if they find the church to be friendly.

2. Follow through with your promises.

If someone volunteers to take a next step in a group, serving or an event, make sure the process is in place to follow up in a timely and personal fashion.

3. Make it easy for people ask questions.

Create a one-stop location, physical or online, where visitors can receive more information about your church.

4. Create ministry environments that compel people to invite their friends.

Excellent preaching and worship music is not enough. Every environment in the church needs to create an opportunity for life change. When that happens, you won't be able to stop folks from inviting their friends.

5. Embrace social media.

Facebook, Twitter and blogs are an easy way to engage people in conversation and develop relationships. As relationships are developed, you'll earn the credibility to encourage people to take next steps.

6. Be different.

Begin an unexpected series, have a unique worship experience or do something (good) that gets people talking.

7. Make your church an active part of the community.

Open your campus to the community, but also get engaged outside the walls of the church where you can directly impact people's lives.

8. Eliminate the noise.

Prioritize what needs to be communicated. Eliminate competing messages. Stop the spam. The fewer messages we deliver, the more likely the important messages will be heard.

9. Encourage word-of-mouth marketing.

The number one reason people will show up to your church for the very first time is because someone invites them. If you have stopped growing, your very first question should be this: *Why have people stopped inviting their friends and what would have to happen for that to change?*

10. Lead by example.

Although leading a church can become all-encompassing, find a way to cultivate personal relationships with nonbelievers.

Tony Morgan is a strategist, writer, speaker and consultant who equips leaders and churches to impact their communities for Christ.

Web: TonyMorganLive.com
Twitter: @TonyMorganLive

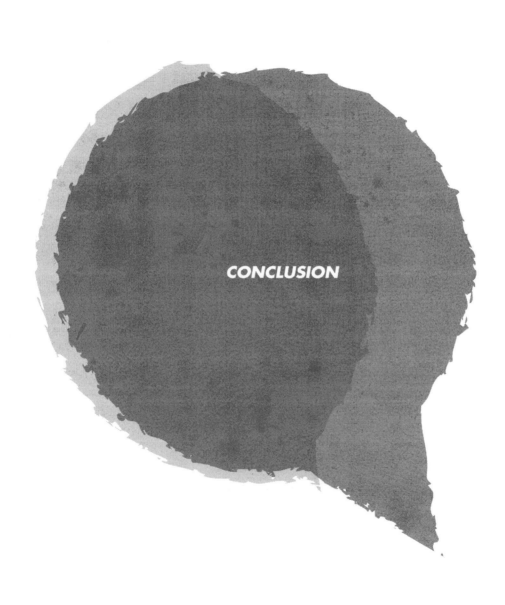

CONCLUSION

Be Outspoken by Tim Schraeder

"God is not a secret to be kept. We're going public with this, as public as a city on a hill. If I make you light-bearers, you don't think I'm going to hide you under a bucket, do you? I'm putting you on a light stand. Now that I've put you there on a hilltop, on a light stand—shine! Keep open house; be generous with your lives. By opening up to others, you'll prompt people to open up with God, this generous Father in heaven." -Matthew 5:14-16,

The Message

We cannot stay silent. When you consider all of the amazing things God has done in each one of our lives and the incredible work he's done in and through our churches, how can we?

Central to our calling as believers is the command to go and tell what we have seen and heard that all men may know the hope we've found in Christ. We cannot stay silent.

Our message is a message of hope in a hopeless world. It's a message of reconciliation in a world filled with strife. It's a message of eternal life. It's a message filled with purpose and destiny, and a message of love, acceptance and grace. It's also a message filled with truth, bringing clarity to confusion and certainty to what seems uncertain.

We have an unprecedented opportunity and it's time for us to be outspoken.

Being outspoken doesn't mean standing on street corners with a bullhorn. It's not doing large-scale marketing blitzes in your community. It's not about selling a slick idea or dressing up the gospel.

Being outspoken means being eager to share our story with the rest of the world by any means possible. It means trying new things while not compromising the integrity of our message. It means being willing to venture into new territory. It's understanding that your church may reach people who may never actually walk through the doors of your church. It means being real and authentic about who you are. It means letting our light shine, being generous with our lives and opening up to others.

Each one of us has the opportunity to help our churches share that story. It's not a secret to be kept but one that must be told again and again in different, creative ways. We've got the greatest story ever told. How will you help your church share it?

We hope you'll choose to be outspoken.

Tim Schraeder has over 10 years of experience leading communications in churches. He is a communications consultant and was previously the director of communications at Park Community Church in Chicago. He's also the instigator of this project and the co-director of the Center for Church Communication.
Web: TimSchraeder.com   **Twitter:** @TimSchraeder

We are a firebrand of communicators, sparking churches to communicate the gospel clearly, effectively and without compromise.

We are made up of passionate change agents, experienced communication professionals and thoughtful instigators; advocating for communicators to find their place in the church—and helping the church get through to their communities so that churches know who they are and are unashamed to tell others.

We identify, resource and celebrate the next generation of church communicators, encouraging them to focus their tenacity and talent for excellent communication, so that churches are sought out by the communities they serve.

We provide smart coaching and mentoring through social media, publishing, events and one-on-one relationships, spotlighting communication that is true, good and beautiful—prompting others to do the same—so that more outsiders become a part of a church community.

We remove barriers to change the way people see Christians and how they speak about the church by promoting relationships, resources, ideas and models for communication. We collaborate people's gifts/skills to work in concert with the creator and their local church.

As God's story comes alive to us and others, we see gospel centered local churches that captivate the attention and liberate the imagination of their community, resulting in more people saying, **"That's what church should be!"**

Center for Church Communication:
Courageous storytellers welcome.

cfcclabs.org

Check out some of our projects:

Church Marketing Sucks
ChurchMarketingSucks.com
The blog to frustrate, educate and motivate the church to communicate, with uncompromising clarity, the truth of Jesus Christ.

Firestarter
cfcclabs.org/labs/knowledge-lab/firestarter/
Celebrating churches that have sparked brilliant communication.

Church Marketing Lab
flickr.com/groups/cfcc/
Show your work, share your feedback.

Local Labs
cfcclabs.org/local/
Meet up with fellow church communicators.

Church Marketing Directory
directory.cfcclabs.org/
Tools, resources and companies that help the church communicate better.

Job Board
jobs.cfcclabs.org/
Find or complete the winning team.

Freelance Board
freelance.cfcclabs.org/
Find or freelance your next project.

Events Calendar
cfcclabs.org/events/
Church communication related events.

Thanks to our many brave contributors:

Brad Abare, Jon Acuff, Maurilio Amorim, Jay Argaet, Ben Arment, Lori Bailey, Dawn Nicole Baldwin, Dave Blanchard, Phil Bowdle, Stephen Brewster, Dawn Bryant, Michael Buckingham, Kerry Bural, Josh Burns, Chad Cannon, Bobby Chandler, Phil Cooke, DJ Chuang, Jon Dale, Nathan Davis, John Dyer, Steve Fogg, Michael Forsberg, Drew Goodmanson, Jim Gray, Danielle Hartland, Kevin D. Hendricks, Scott Hodge, Blaine Hogan, Adam Jeske, Bianca Juarez-Olthoff, Matt Knisely, Charles Lee, Jan Lynn, Will Mancini, Vince Marotte, Cheryl Marting, Evan McBroom, Scott McClellan, Kem Meyer, Tony Morgan, Eric Murrell, Cleve Persinger, Jesse Phillips, Stephen Proctor, John Saddington, Jeremy Scheller, Tim Schraeder, Jennifer Schuchmann, Jeremy Sexton, Kent Shaffer, Curtis Simmons, Cameron Smith, Rhett Smith, Paul Steinbrueck, Tony Steward, Katie Strandlund, Leonard Sweet, Gerry True, Corbyn Tyson, K.C. Walsh, Denny Weinman, Justin Wise, Shawn Wood and Jason Yarborough.

Thanks to the team that pulled this book together: Tim Schraeder, Kevin Hendricks, Michael Buckingham, Brian Alexander, and the many people who shared ideas, offered insights, gave feedback and pointed out typos (thanks Mom!).

Thanks to the many people who spread the word about this book. You're likely reading this book not because of our marketing efforts, but because of someone else who shared it with you. Tell 'em we said thanks.

Thanks to you the reader for getting this far. If you liked what you read, pass it on.

Thanks to the pastors and communicators struggling to tell the greatest story ever told. Thanks to the church for being the community where that story is lived out. And thanks be to God for loving us and giving us a story that demands we be outspoken.

Tim Schraeder Thanks...

Immense thanks to John King, lead pastor at Riverside Community Church in Peoria, Ill., for giving an 18 year old kid who had passion for the local church and some poor design the skills a chance. Thanks to Eric Robbins for showing me how to use PageMaker and to Chad Fagerland for teaching me God could use anyone to build the church. Huge thanks to friends and mentors along the way: Kirt Manuel, Kem Meyer, Dawn Nicole Baldwin and Shawn Wood. And, to a few people who have inspired me: Seth Godin, Jason Fried and Steven Pressfield. Thanks to all who contribued to and supported this project from its ideation to completion — this was a team effort. Thanks for lending your words and ideas to create something for our tribe!

Made in the USA
Charleston, SC
29 December 2011